BUILDING WEALTH USING THE TIN CAN METHOD

MARGARETTE PERKINS

BUILDING WEALTH USING THE TIN CAN METHOD by Margarette Perkins
Published by Creation House Press
600 Rinehart Road
Lake, Mary, FL 32746

All rights reserved. No portion of this book may be reproduced, stored in a retrieval system, or transmitted in any form or by any means—electronic, mechanical, photocopy, recording, or any other—except for brief quotations in printed reviews, without the prior permission of the publisher.

Unless otherwise indicated, all Scripture quotations are from the King James Version of the Bible.

Scripture quotations marked AMP are from the Amplified Bible. Old Testament copyright © 1965, 1987 by the Zondervan Corporation. The Amplified New Testament copyright © 1954, 1958, 1987 by the Lockman Foundation. Used by permission.

Scripture quotations marked NIV are from the Holy Bible, New International Version. Copyright © 1973, 1978, 1984, International Bible Society. Used by permission.

Scripture quotations marked NKJV are from the New King James Version of the Bible. Copyright © 1979, 1980, 1982 by Thomas Nelson Inc., publishers. Used by permission.

Scripture quotations marked NLT are from the Holy Bible, New Living Translation, copyright © 1996. Used by permission of Tyndale House Publishers, Inc., Wheaton, IL 60189. All rights reserved.

Copyright © 1998 by Margarette Perkins
All rights reserved
ISBN: 0-88419-561-9
Library of Congress Catalog Card Number: 98-74502

8 9 0 1 2 3 4 BVG 6 5 4 3 2 1
Printed in the United States of America

Acknowledgments

At first my acknowledgments were going to read, "Thanks to everyone who made this book possible." But my heart would not let me do it. *You* deserve better than that—and you shall have better.

When I was inspired to write this book in 1994, if I had known what the physical and mental stress my body would sustain, I'm certain I would have closed shop. I can't count the times I've put it down, feeling unsure and unqualified, and thinking, *Who... me—Margarette—write a book about my financial lifestyle? Girl, you're an entrepreneur—not a writer. How silly of you!* But the encouragement and the life-changing experiences of my many friends and colleagues who benefitted from it gave me the desire to not give up.

I acknowledge those who saw in me what, at times, I couldn't see in myself. Their prayers kept hope alive. They believed in me, which caused me to believe even more in myself. So, to you I'm forever grateful. Your prayers and support made it happen.

To my dear and only sister, Mary, and brother-in-law Thomas, who are too proud of me to speak—and have withstood all my good, bad, and ugly times—Thanks, thanks, thanks!

To Maria Tillery, whom God allowed to be transformed from *rags to riches* through this message and method.

To Jimmy and Linda Haythe, who before the book began, said, "Write it; put it in a book." You never gave up on me.

To Anne, whom God used to confirm the need for the rich and famous to hear this message.

To Bernice and my CCN family, who were bold enough to establish the first forum for this message to be taught.

To Pastor Chris and Sharon, who believed this message enough to allow me to teach it to their congregation.

To my financial advisor, Mr. Willie Reese, and firm, who stood in *awe* of my method of accumulation and who did the "foot" and "heart" work in finding a publisher. Surely I can call you "friend."

To Irene Perry, who so many times has been *a light* to me in the basement.

To the Wilkins, for their many hours of prayer and labor in a multiplicity of ways to help me bring this project to completion. Thanks for your endurance.

To Joyce and Ruthleen, who prayed and gave their ears to hear my ups and downs.

To Bishop Mack and Brenda Timberlake and Bishop Eddie Long for taking time out of your busy schedules to read the book and then write forewords. I'm most grateful.

To Tom Freiling, who initiated the publishing process at Creation House Press.

To Dave Welday and all the Creation House Press staff, and to you, Barbara Dycus—whose words ring loud, "Margarette, it's a good book!" Thanks, I needed to hear that (from an editor's point of view).

To Tina Moore and Mary Grant who laboriously typed, retyped, and typed some more with a smile, giving me encouragement to keep going, yet making me smile as the message changed both of you into butterflies.

To Rheuben and Niva, thanks for your endless support.

To Bishop John Neal and First Lady Wanda and the Agape Christian Faith Center in Landstuhl, Germany, who believed so much in the message that they opened their doors for me to launch it in Europe. You know I love you right back!

To all my family, including those special loved ones in heaven, resting in the bosom of the Lord.

Above all, to my beloved, beautiful daughter, Porcelain, who has suffered more than any. You have seen my tears and shared my pain from day one. You endured my neglect of you in many areas throughout the writing process, yet loved me just the same and allowed me to finish. Baby, God and the message in this book will reward you and your children's children for many years to come. Remember, you are the answer to the faith prayer that I prayed thirteen years ago. I love you.

To You, God, I owe all.

CONTENTS

Foreword
    by Bishop Eddie Long. vi
Foreword
    by Bishop Mack Timberlake, Jr. vii
Preface ix
Introduction xii
1. Why Save? 1
2. God's Financial Academy 24
3. The Devourer of the Out-of-Order 53
4. The Power of Obedience 69
5. The Birth of the Tin Can. 82
6. Go to the Ant. 97
7. Reasons Not to Trust Man 114
8. Interest From Hell. 131
9. Fees From Hell. 144
10. Excusers, Abusers, and Misusers 165
11. A Tin Can for the Rich and Famous? 199
12. The Golden Rule 218

Foreword by Bishop Eddie Long

One of the missing links in our communities is the understanding of Proverbs 13:22: "A good man leaveth an inheritance to his children's children: and the wealth of the sinner is laid up for the just." We have to understand that a good or a righteous person leaves his descendants an inheritance with which to operate and to carry out God's kingdom agenda in their generation.

Building Wealth Using the Tin Can Method offers practical, down-to-earth, biblically based financial advice to the reader. Using a rich understanding of current events and the economic climate of this nation, Margarette Perkins walks the reader through a plan that is simple yet effective. Easy to read, understand, and implement, this book offers applicable money management to anyone bold enough to give God a try.

I thank God that there are still those in the body of Christ, like Margarette Perkins, who can take current situations, apply the Word of God, and help others not only to gain an understanding, but to have an opportunity to make God's Word apply to the here and now. It is inspiring and refreshing to see that the Holy Spirit still places a desire in the hearts of others to help in the way that the author blessed me—and will bless you as well.

—Eddie L. Long, D.D., D.H.L.
Senior Pastor, New Birth Missionary Baptist Church

Foreword by Bishop Mack Timberlake, Jr.

What we think about money is often what we think about life. Money is the power part of the world. How we handle finances determines the negative or positive impact of it in our lives.

Building Wealth Using the Tin Can Method is a book full of wisdom, practical as well as spiritual, concerning financial success.

The truths of this book are the real down-to-earth facts that send a wake-up call to individuals as well as nations. Money is ready to do good or evil according to the owner's discretion.

Explore the benefits of *Building Wealth Using the Tin Can Method,* and pass this excellent method on to another to insure a generation of blessings.

—Dr. Mack Timberlake, Jr.
Senior Pastor, Christian Faith Center
Creedmoor, North Carolina

When I was asked to write a few words for Margarette's book, *Building Wealth Using the Tin Can Method,* I felt honored. Margarette is not only a friend, but she is also a client. The information that has been written by Margarette has been a life experience for her, and she shares some great revelations that God gave her to put in this book.

The time I have been working with Margarette has been very fruitful and rewarding, because I have seen fantastic results. When I first met Margarette, and she began to explain some of her techniques of saving to me, I found it very fascinating—because she makes it seem so simple.

You have to understand my background in financial planning—when she made this technique seem so simple and understandable, I knew she had something special. The most important thing about her technique is that it has worked for her. In all of my days working in the financial arena, I had not seen anyone who truly knew how to save money—and stuck with it.

I believe this book is a "must-read" for people all over the world who have the desire to turn their pennies into millions. The tin can method is, without question, a method that mothers and fathers can use to teach their children.

—WILLIE REESE, FINANCIAL PLANNER
W.W. MANAGEMENT GROUP TRUST

PREFACE

Let's cut to the chase, Americans—Christians and non-Christians alike are savings poor, and future unsure. They are being legally robbed in one way or the other by the system—and are robbing themselves as well.

Too many believe the system is going to put them in comfortable rocking chairs when their time for retirement arrives. Get a grip and read my lips—"It ain't gonna happen." Man's system cannot be depended upon. The system is out of order and in debt just as you are. That's why they are pressing you hard financially to bail them out, without displaying financial accountability. Pay attention to the financial tremors and stop believing the news media's version of the truth. Desystemitize yourself. *That's a prophetic warning!* Only a miracle can lead this world system out of financial woes—and only God can hand out miracles. And I propose to that you turn to Him.

God's truths are simple, but with simplicity comes order. God *is* and always will be a God of order. However one must utilize the unlocking key. If you follow His order, you will find the key that will unlock all His hidden and unhidden treasure. This key will show you how to lay a solid foundation on which you can begin to **build your wealth.**

Probably today you're living paycheck to paycheck,

BUILDING WEALTH USING THE TIN CAN METHOD

constantly worrying about your future and the future of your family. God never intended for you to just barely survive—but man's system does. Most people never break free from the bondage of poverty because they don't understand how to do so. For many years I struggled, just getting by, never saving or preparing for the future, until I discovered the unlocking key.

If you are as I was, you're always interested in TV infomercials, newspaper ads, or financial seminars that promise financial freedom—but at a cost of $1,000 and more. If you're like me, you can't afford them. So now what do you do?

But that's all right. What you'll read in this book is better. You won't have to spend a fortune to learn how to amass a fortune to secure your future. In this book, which you can purchase for less than twenty dollars, I will explain how to simply *respect* and *save*—by raising your consciousness in how to deal with and respect your *present income* to insure your *future income*. I've learned through my trials and errors, that *making* it is one thing—*keeping* it is another. And that's where this book will chart your course.

My plan is proven by my own experience—as well as by the experience of others. For me, I realized that before I could *invest*, I needed to *nest*, or I would have nothing to invest. Investing requires money. So before you can *grow* you must *sow*. Building a little wealth can be simple and easy.

Before you start investing, first read this book. Read it from cover to cover to receive its full benefits. Read it with a pen and a highlighter. Don't just read it—think about it; pray about it. See if it will raise your awareness, speak to your negligence, and develop your mind-set. It'll cause you to think in a manner that you may have never thought of before. Yet the message and method is simple.

Although this book is not about investing (stocks, bonds, and so forth), do understand that I am in favor of investing.

PREFACE

But nest (secure and save) first, otherwise you'll have nothing to invest. Therefore, s*aving* is the focus of this book; How to start saving and what to start with. The wealth-building foundation you will learn is absent in the lives of most Americans and non-Americans; Christians and non-Christians.

People, the new wave of the future is to save for the future so as not to become a slave in the future. In order to change your *present* condition, you must change your *thinking* condition, which will change your *financial* condition.

It's high time to take charge of your finances and to live the life you've been dreaming about. Read on, and here's to your financial health and wealth. Build it using the tin can method.

—MARGARETTE PERKINS

Introduction

What are you willing to do to change and elevate your present lifestyle? What are you willing to do to make tomorrow, next week, next year, or even ten years from now different from today? The Word says, "As a man thinketh, so is he" (Prov. 23:7). It all starts with changing your mind-set and your present way of thinking and doing.

And if you can think, you can act. If you act, you can change your *present* financial condition! If you work towards changing your financial condition, you can *and will* change your lifestyle.

Thankfully, *you are ready* for change or you wouldn't be reading this book. Though this books is about saving it is also about rendering one's *first fruits* unto God, for without this ingredient no *lasting* fortune will be solidly and securely established or enjoyed. It's funny how many have no problem pledging allegiance to a flag, but refuse to pledge allegiance to God or His order. A flag is dead—It can't help you. but God is alive and holds plans and strategies that can set the captives free!

Therefore this book is written to raise your consciousness about God and His financial system, the finance systems of this world, and your place in both of them—particularly in the area of savings. It is my aim to inspire you to choose your *only* and *last* hope—God—and His financial system,

Introduction

because Satan's system has been ruthlessly devouring America, including much of the church.

The exorbitant interest rates that Satan's world system has exacted on those who take his loans have thrown America into an indebtedness that is running out of control. Savings are low, and interest is high. Most Americans are simply trying to survive—including those in God's household of faith.

God hasn't called His people merely to survive. He has called us to overcome in prosperity in order to finance His work on earth. The area of accumulated savings is one He seeks to apply to the work of His church in the earth. So savings will be a major emphasis throughout this book. But we will also look at some economic realities you may never have taken the time to consider.

Two of the realities we will examine are the major culprits that today are robbing America's people of potential savings. They are:

1. *The faults of our system*—including legalized stealing in various arenas; excessive and increasing taxation; ridiculous and increasing interest, fees, and nonsensical governmental spending.

2. *The faults of one's self*—including disobedience, mismanagement, and ridiculous adverse consumption.

Each of these culprits must be attacked with tenacity to evoke a change and reverse the double curse spoken of in Malachi 3. We will look at this curse in great detail.

THE FAULTS OF OUR SYSTEM

The first culprit demands an eye-opening corporate response from "we the people." God at work in people is the only force and power that *will* evoke change and redirect our great nation. We the people have the power to establish a change, but only if we the people utilize that power.

According to recent surveys, fewer people (especially baby boomers) are adequately saving for their families' future. The much talked-about coming boom in the over-65 age population, coupled with the failing social security program and the uncertainty of other entitlement programs, will receive much attention in this book.

You must begin to save more to insure *your own* personal welfare and safeguard your future. Dependency upon God, and ourselves, demands attention.

Sad to say, our government will not and cannot be trusted any longer to deal fairly with the American people. It wastes hundred of billions of dollars yearly. Far too much money is being taken from us in taxes, fees, and by other unreasonable methods. Many live in fear of a government audit whereby they could be ordered to gather up years of financial records for review—only to be penalized out of house and home. Recent IRS hearings reveal a frightening government system that preys upon honest citizens who have either fallen on bad times, made honest mistakes, or made no mistakes at all.

Because of the excessive amounts of interest connected to our national debts, the American government has become a dangerous force today, which is driving many of its people into doom and gloom. Many are personally abusing their money by wasting it on so-called pleasures that are detrimental to both their health and wealth. Millions of potential savings dollars are filtering away, their loss justified by the cliché—"I can't or never will."

Many households have "zero" savings coupled with a "zero" concern and a "zero" mentality for their own welfare. Because of this, you will read about the need to commit to God's order through obedience in this book over and over again. Some chapters are brief. Others are not. The message may even seem redundant at times, but purposely so, for what one hears or reads constantly is usually not forgotten. I pray the message of this book evokes a positive change in your life.

The Faults of One's Self

The second savings-stealing culprit—our own disobedience—will be dealt with in this book through God's written Word as well. One must learn to apply the oracles of God in order to experience Him as Master Multiplier. God must first have something to multiply. He wants to give us the thirtyfold, sixtyfold, and hundredfold-plus returns, but He must have something from us to give in return. If you give Him nothing, He can only multiply nothing, and in the end you will have an abundance of nothing. Great amounts of money are being made, but very little is being saved—and far too little is being accounted for.

Many will think this message is too simple or that it won't work and therefore won't apply it to their lives. *Saving pennies, nickels, and dimes after giving God your tithes?* Sounds too simple. What about stocks? Stocks are always out there, and God can tell you when to buy—that is once He trusts you. He knows where the **good deals** are and wants to send you to buy them at just the right time. And He wants to buy them through your hands for pennies compared to what the world would normally charge.

So I beg to differ with those who say this message is too simple. Simple things are just that—simple. *But simple things can be profound*. A simple black dress with a strand of pearls can make as powerful a statement—or more—than a dress that cost thousands of dollars. Half dollars and dollars add up to thousands if constantly amassed and compounded. So never prejudge anything by its size. Start small if that is all you can do, and be thankful—because if you work it, it will work for you.

Building Wealth Using the Tin Can Method

Oseola McCarty, a God-fearing woman, is a wonderful message-sender to this nation of the value of small beginnings. Oseola saved $150,000 on a salary earned by washing other people's laundry. Remember—it's not how much one *makes,* but how much one *saves.* If Ms. McCarty can do it, so can you. I guarantee that she didn't despise small beginnings. Many applaud her generosity for giving her savings to fund scholarships for students. But I believe she should receive more applause for her ability to **save** and amass this money on her **small** salary. *Without the saving there could have been no giving.*

I believe the tables will soon turn on the *wealthy wicked.* They will find themselves off the world's Fortune 500 list as God establishes His own Fortune 500+ list. I speak this prophetically: Before the time of the end when the Antichrist strongarms the financial systems during his tribulation reign, many worldly corporations will see the dwindling of their resources as their assets flood into the church. God will move on the hearts of the world's wealthy wicked to offer inexplicable deals to God's righteous in the church.

Many wealthy people will receive Jesus and commit their resources to God's work in the earth. The businesses of unrepentant businessmen and women will be judged, and the profits once used to line their own pockets will be inexplicably released to the work of the church. "The wealth of the sinner is laid up for the just" (Prov. 13:22); the days of this scripture's fulfillment is certainly upon us.

Those in government who have plundered honest, hardworking citizens (and you will learn of them in this book) will be judged. So will businessmen who have burdened their employees through downsizing and greed-based layoffs. The church will be blessed and will take center stage as we climb from *rags to riches*—in some cases literally overnight. Witty inventions and supernaturally increased investments will catapult many into what the world calls "overnight successes." But their successes derive from their obedience. The world will be astonished and will have to acknowledge the amazing progression of events as a direct result of a sovereign move of God. As a result, many will be saved.

God wants to lead His children out of financial calamity. He led the children of Israel by the rod of Moses, and He will lead you today. Those who are obedient and in order are able already to do more with $50 sown into the kingdom of God than the disobedient can do with $50,000—and their power is about to increase explosively. God will cause miraculous favor to come upon His people and will intertwine that favor with their finances, producing supernatural miracles.

New revelation is being imparted to men and women in the area of biblical finance today. Through creativity and inspiration, God is teaching these men and women to lead His people out of financial bondage. I believe I am one of these anointed ones. So it will be my purpose in this book to recite the commands of God and set them ablaze in your memory. *Those who have ears, let them hear.*

Note: Even our president and national leaders are hinting that savings must be enhanced by the American people. The new wave of the future is to save for the future.

President Clinton, left, with Al Gore, center, and Newt Gingrich, fear that baby boomers could wipe out Social Security.

WASHINGTON—Saying Americans' erratic retirement saving habits are a threat to future generations, President Clinton on Thursday asked Congress to make Social Security reform its first order of business next year "so we baby boomers don't bankrupt our children."

He [Gingrich] said the key to salvaging Social Security lies in restructuring the FICA payroll tax. He said American probably save very little now because the tax takes such a big bite out of their paychecks.

"It is an automatic regressive tax," Gingrich said. "We have to preserve and protect [Social Security] but at the same time, we have to be honest about its impact. Lower taxes is inevitably good for savings."

Excerpt taken from "Political leaders mull Social Secuirty bind" The News & Observer, Friday, June 5, 1998, The Associated Press.

ONE
WHY SAVE?

Learn to detest the stench of poverty and lack. They have a smell of their own, and far too many have become familiar and comfortable with their odor.

Do not despise... small beginnings.
—Zechariah 4:10, NLT

To most people, tin is a cheap, worthless piece of metal. But it's far from being worthless or useless—just as this tin can message is neither worthless nor useless.

Tin is a white metallic element people have used since ancient times. The earliest known use of tin occurred about 3500 B.C. in a southern city in Mesopotamia called Ur, which was located in the region we know today as modern Iraq. The people of Ur made tools and weapons from bronze, an alloy of tin and copper. As you read this message, you will realize that the *tin can wealth-building method* will serve you as a tool and a weapon. Yes, as a tool and weapon to fight in the war against disobedience and lack. It will also serve you as a financial fortress and defense system.

Tin is very malleable and can easily be formed into various shapes that enable it to be better utilized. Tin is used today in the manufacture of a wide variety of products that

Building Wealth Using the Tin Can Method

allow millions of people to live bountiful and better lives.

Just like the element tin, the tin can method, if used properly, can also provide a variety of good uses. You will learn that a little bit of savings (to start) will go a long way. Tin provides a higher standard of living and economic elevation for society in general. How many women or restaurants worldwide could imagine life without moisture-proof wrapping, which is tin formed into extremely thin foil? Tin is used to make stannous flouride (tin plus flouride), which aids in preventing tooth decay. Tin is also a protector. It protects the steel in cans from rust and gives the cans an attractive appearance. It prevents weak acids in food from damaging the inside of cans.

Tin is also a preservative. The word *preservative* or *preserve* means **"to save, conserve, maintain, secure, rescue, defend, safeguard, shield, can, prevent decay and to keep alive."** All of these definitions are used repeatedly throughout this book in some form. All of these utilizations of tin—and of the tin can message—aid in combating loss and producing a level of success and manageability. Tin is not a luxury metal or ingredient—*but most certainly is a necessary item or element.* So is the tin can method! Not a luxury method, but a necessary one if you want to improve your financial condition.

Here's my point—manufacturers improve the properties of various metals by adding **small** amounts of tin. Not large amounts, but *small* amounts. This is the principle required to start your tin can savings: You don't need to have a large amount, just a *small* amount.

Because tin is so disposable, most people throw out tin items when they're finished with them, just as many dispose of their paychecks in various nonproductive ways.

So the utilization of tin and this message are synonymous with one another. Without tin, our lives would greatly lessen. Just as they lessen without obedience and order, which are the **main ingredients** of this tin can method.

It doesn't take much to begin a savings once you get in order. With just a *small* amount, God can improve your lifestyle and financial status miraculously.

The small amounts of tin that find their way into our lives daily are life protectors and enhancers. This is where I will strike my parallel with the tin can savings message of this book.

Excuses, Excuses

Americans live in one of the richest countries in the world. Yet many who read this book may have worked half a lifetime with nothing to show for it. Today's median household income is about $31,200, but only about 4.9 percent of this amount—the lowest percentage of any industrialized nation—is saved. Americans owe more than $1 trillion. More than one million Americans file for personal bankruptcy every year. And 15 percent of the U. S. population is currently living below the poverty level.

We who live in the United States have many excuses for our nonsaving ways. Believing a large amount of money is needed to start saving is a major excuse. In the following pages I will show why this isn't true.

Every person should start—with pennies if they have to—to leave a financial inheritance to their children's children. We should love our children enough to do this. The Word of God clearly states in Proverbs 13:22 that a good man will leave an inheritance for his children's children. This will allow the next generation to continue financing the gospel while allowing God to meet their needs and desires in return.

With all of this in mind, how can we measure up to this important mandate? How can we accomplish such a task when many Christians and non-Christians alike are in such a mess regarding their finances?

Building Wealth Using the Tin Can Method

Choose to Think

To start, we must choose to think. Throughout this book I'm going to ask you to put on your thinking cap, elevate your mind-set, and start thinking about some things—obvious and not so obvious—that most just gloss right over. So begin measuring up right now by taking a mental assessment. Start where you are by tallying up what you have to leave as an inheritance should you die tomorrow. Maybe like many, you will realize you don't have much of an inheritance, *if any,* to leave to the next generation. Most people can't afford to miss even one day from work and are one or two paychecks away from being broke or filing for bankruptcy. So it is important to think **now** and to think ahead.

==Saving requires obedience, discipline, good planning, and prayer==. It must be a continual habit if we are to see the Scriptures manifested in our lives. Discipline and clarity of thought must come to the forefront. Forget the excuse that it's too late for you, because it isn't.

It's Never Too Late for a New Beginning

Tin can thinking says to begin by **starting** now. Start fresh and leave the past behind you. Remember that God is a redeemer of the time. He will restore to you all that you have lost or have allowed to be stolen once you obey His word. Commit yourself to get back on track. Hebrews 4:15–16 in the Amplified Version makes this principle clearer and more personal:

> For we do not have a High Priest Who is unable to understand and sympathize and have a fellow feeling with our weaknesses and infirmities and liability to the assaults of temptation, but One Who has been tempted in every respect as we are, yet without sinning. Let us

> then fearlessly and confidently and boldly draw near to the throne of grace—the throne of God's unmerited favor [to us sinners]; that we may receive mercy [for our failures] and find grace to help in good time for every need—appropriate help and well-timed help, coming just when we need it.

God knows all too well that we have missed the mark. But He is always there for us. He will never forsake us. And He always makes a way of escape for those who have missed the mark, just as He consistently made a way for the apostle Paul. Learn from your mistakes, shake the dust off your feet, and keep on going. There's no use in "crying over spilled milk," as we say.

Paul pressed forward. He pressed toward the mark of a higher calling in Christ Jesus. He knew that the only way to redeem lost time in view of his past mistakes was through Christ Jesus. And so it will be with you. But you must know that only Christ can help you do this.

God always has a Plan B when we've failed Plan A. That's why He's called our Redeemer. When man missed the mark with the Old Covenant (and God knew we would), God sent His Son Jesus with a new and better covenant, composed of better principles and promises. God is always equipped and ready with better improvements and plans. That's true today—He hasn't changed. We must simply ask and do our part.

When you're feeling down and out, just say, "I can do all things through Christ who strengthens me" (Phil. 4:13, NKJV). Remember the words "all things," because you can. And remember that He is the one who is strengthening you to do all things if you sincerely desire His help. God is a redeemer of the times. He redeemed us from the curse of the law, and He will redeem you from the curse of your past financial mistakes when you choose to get in order and work with Him on His plan for your life. Why? Because

Building Wealth Using the Tin Can Method

God is a God of the second chance.

God can take all your past mistakes and failures in the area of finances and fashion them overnight to fulfill the destiny of your life. He can help you leave an inheritance to your children that seemed impossible when you first started reading this chapter. God is not slack with His promises. It gives Him good pleasure to give gifts to His children. He desires so much for you to be the head and not the tail—His Word says so. He desires that you lend and never borrow. And when you line yourself up with His Word, you will see His Word manifested in your life. He will make you ruler over much once you become a good steward over what He has already given you.

I repeat, God can change your financial status overnight. All the silver and gold belongs to Him. In fact, "the earth is the Lord's, and the fulness thereof; the world, and they that dwell therein" (Ps. 24:1). God is waiting on you! So line up and get in order with His Word. He won't work miracles on your behalf if you're not in order—because He is a God of order, which is established in His Word. He will always be a God of order. His order will not change, because God changes not. That's why 1 Corinthians 14:40 tells us to do things decently and in order.

Please, **get in order.** The tin can message is God's message of order. Obey His words and commandments, and His promises will surely follow. God is not slack with His promises, and neither does He lie. It doesn't require an arm or a leg for you to start repositioning yourself. What is required is that you **start now,** today, immediately while you read this book. **Today,** not tomorrow, is the day of salvation (2 Cor. 6:2). Don't put off until tomorrow what you need to do today. Please!

Prepare for the Unexpected

Another reason to start saving today is to prepare for the

WHY SAVE?

unexpected. As long as Satan lives, emergencies and unexpected events will occur. Some we can control, others we can't. However, emergencies, regardless of their nature, are at least more digestible when one has money set aside that is accessible. It is not wise to think that someone will always come to your rescue when an emergency appears. Many people who have money will not always have a desire to assist you.

Remember the saying, "Sister, brother, mama, daddy may have, but bless the child who has his own"? In many cases, this is certainly true. Not only will your own accessible money ease the pain of an emergency, but it will save you the embarrassment of having others know your financial hardship. Money, whether you have some or not, is a very *personal* matter.

Five years ago my husband passed away tragically and unexpectedly. Prior to his death my daughter and I wanted for little. We were accustomed to a certain lifestyle, which included many fine things. In addition to the normal everyday expenses, our lifestyle included a yard man, a housekeeper, the constant needs of an ever-maturing child, and continuous travel. We required much money.

After his death, my husband's income could no longer be depended upon. The concerns of maintaining a household normally weigh heavily on the mind of a surviving spouse. But because of earlier preparations, there were no pressing concerns for my daughter and I. We didn't even need to depend upon the provisions of an insurance policy payoff. Being in order spared us the kind of embarrassment I mentioned earlier of having to ask others for money.

When a loved one dies, most family members are wonderful and respectful. But no matter how wonderful extended family are, if their purses can't help you (especially if finances are needed), sympathy is all their heart will be able to contribute.

Friends and family may even avoid visiting a grieving

family member if they suspect financial assistance is needed after some tragedy. One of the best beforehand preparations anyone can make is to be positioned squarely in God's *financial order.* When this is the case and mishaps occur, you can rest in knowing that God (unlike some people) will never leave or forsake you.

OUT-OF-ORDER CATASTROPHES

Natural disasters are another reason we should save. Do you realize that one unexpected catastrophe could wipe you out? I was reading a local newspaper one morning while I was eating breakfast and came across an article related to Hurricane Bertha. Bertha hit a farmer's crop in the Brunswick County area in 1996. The farmer stated that he thought that year was going to be his best ever. His crops were tall and ready for harvest, and the ears of corn were the biggest he had ever seen. The commodities markets were cooperating with expected record-high prices for tobacco and corn. But listen to his next statement: "All that changed in just two hours when the storm roared through my fields ripping 340 acres of tobacco and leveling 200 acres of corn."

Catastrophe happened to him, and it could happen to you. And, God forbid, if it does, who is the only one who could redeem you? Only God, our redeemer. Yes, only He can redeem the time and our catastrophes. That's why it is important that we be in order and know the Lord when catastrophes present themselves.

When the stock market crashed on "Black Monday," many were stripped of millions and billions of dollars in the blink of an eye. Many lost their minds as well as their stamina. Some committed suicide. In whom did they put their trust? It wasn't God. I will often refer to this scripture in Jeremiah: "Cursed be the man that trusteth in man [mammon world systems]...Blessed is the man that trusteth in the Lord" (Jer. 17:5, 7).

WHY SAVE?

I'm sure if stockholders had an inkling of an idea concerning what was to come—like our recent stock market fall—some form of preparation would have been made. But we don't know...we can't know...we're not omniscient—only God is. That's why He commands us to trust and rely on Him. Blessed be those who do.

So get in order and expect God to keep His end of the bargain. When you do, you'll find that He watches over His Word to perform it. You can take the promises of God to the bank!

When you learn to trust God, your financial condition will turn around. So will your attitude and thinking process. Little by little...bit by bit.

And if by chance the enemy chooses to perch on your shoulders and whisper negative thoughts like, "You're stupid to save a penny, nickel, a dime, or even a dollar..." just tell him, "Get back!" And when he goes on to whisper, "As expensive as things are today, that little bit of money you want to save isn't going to help you...it will never grow or amass into anything. You may as well spend it! Wait until you get a thousand dollars and then save," tell him again, "Satan, get back! You are a liar. I've listened too long to you. that's why I don't have a savings.

If you let him, Satan will convince you that you'll never get that thousand dollars. Why? So you will become discouraged and never start. Satan knows better than you that God's promises are true, and that you will never listen to his lies again if you ever discover otherwise. He doesn't want money in Christians' hands, especially obedient ones. He knows we will use it to spread the gospel and tear his kingdom down.

So stop listening to Satan's nonsense. He doesn't have your best interests in mind. Just remind the devil what the Word says in John 8:44:

> You were a murderer from the beginning, and abode

Building Wealth Using the Tin Can Method

not in the truth, because there is no truth in you. When you speaketh a lie, you speaketh of your own: for you are a liar, and the father of it.

Now remind the devil of what the Word says in Malachi 3:11:

I will rebuke the devourer for your sakes, and he shall not destroy the fruits of your ground: neither shall your vine cast her fruit before the time in the field, saith the Lord of hosts.

Now, challenge the devourer with the Word and say:

- "God is a master multiplier!"
- "God gives the increase!"
- "I will not despise small beginnings!"
- "I plant, God waters, and the harvest comes up in due season!"
- "Besides devil, listening to you is the reason I don't have any savings now—and the buck stops here! I am starting today. Get thee behind me, Satan, in the name of Jesus!"

Good for you! See how easy it was for you to put Satan back into his rightful place? But remember this, although he may be gone for a season, he will reappear for sure. And when he does, all you need to do is give him the same dosages of truth you did the time before, until he realizes that you are more serious about this than he believes. Let him know *daily* that you're on the road to financial recovery!

Remember this golden nugget and rehearse it over and over until it sinks deep down in your spirit: God knows where all the good deals are. When God directed me to save, I too asked the question, "Why save?"

And God said, *"Because I know where all the good deals*

are. And when they are revealed, you'll need some funds."

As I pondered that, the Holy Spirit elaborated even more concerning this matter. That *simple* answer had an even more powerful meaning than I could have ever imagined or perceived. Yes, God gives thirtyfold, sixtyfold, and a hundred-plus-fold returns. He is a master multiplier. And when I don't have what it takes to buy a house, car, or a boat…His supernatural power will produce what only He can do—**produce a miracle!**

Now, start thinking about getting a tin can. And when you do, don't forget to anoint it with oil along with your small change and dollars while you make a vow unto God; then start. Tell Him that you're going to change your negative financial condition through obedience to His Word. Then throw your loose change and dollar bills from your pockets, wallet, or purse into the can.

Remember, it was a small, smooth stone that David used to kill old Goliath (1 Sam. 17). And it was that little bit of oil that kept the widow woman, her son, and the prophet alive (1 Kings 17). A beginning savings may be all that God needs to produce your miracle, too.

> **THINK ABOUT IT—**
> HAVE YOU IDENTIFIED LATELY THE RESOURCES THAT GOD HAS ENTRUSTED TO YOU? UNLESS YOU UTILIZE HIS METHOD OF ORDER, YOU WON'T EXPERIENCE HIS MAXIMUM KINGDOM RETURN.

PUT ON YOUR THINKING CAP—DILIGENCE OR LUCK?

Now that you have your thinking cap on, think about this: Have you heard needy or financially lacking people say about the rich: "They're just lucky. Fate has been good to them"? Or, "Money always seems to follow them because of God's favor"? Yet the Word says God is no respecter of persons. Can you explain to me why an astronaut knows so much about the stars while you don't? Simply because he has applied himself to study and learn about them—and you haven't. He has mastered that in which he was interested. He's now an expert in his professional endeavor. So it can be with your financial endeavors.

> Study to shew thyself approved unto God, a workman that needeth not to be ashamed, rightly dividing the word of truth.
> —2 Timothy 2:15

Those who make the grade to be astronauts apply themselves to study and know about flight, navigation, space, and the stars. The reason we pay doctors and lawyers so much is because of the dedication and care they spent in acquiring their skills and knowledge. You pay them for knowledge that you don't have.

It isn't luck or fate that puts the astronaut in space or the doctor and lawyer in practice. They had a desire, and they pursued their dreams. They mastered that in which they were interested. And the same is true about finances. If you're interested in them, you can master them, because God is no respecter of persons.

THREE ECONOMIC LOCALES

There are three economic locations in which people live. In which one are you presently residing?

1. The county of economic lack
2. The county of economically even
3. The county of economic plenty

If you're presently living within the *county of economic lack,* you're there because that's where you've chosen to live. You may not have had anything to do with what put you there if you were born into it, but it's been your choice to stay there.

If you're currently living in the *county of economically even,* you're probably there because you made a choice to relocate out of the county of economic lack.

The *county of economic plenty* is where we all want to be. Once there we say, "Why did it take me so long?" Once we move there, we realize that the knowledge to get there was always available to us.

WHERE ARE YOU LIVING?

The tin can method of financial accountability will teach you to take stock of what you have and where you're living financially so you can relocate to where you truly want to be. Many people have no idea of where they stand concerning their finances. So they need to get serious. Many husbands and wives have a combined income that is much greater than they realize. But many suffer from financial communication breakdowns and are unaware of the small things that daily eat away at their funds. Many have no savings plan and waste much of what they make.

If this is you, start learning to communicate. The Word says, "It is the little foxes that spoil the vine" (Song of Sol. 2:15). A penny is a little coin in the monetary system, yet when it is consistently saved it can amass and become much. When you or your spouse say, "I can't save," a little fox is spoiling your vine because of your words.

Your tongue is a little member that can cause great financial good or harm. When you listen to negative verbal withdrawals about your abilities and capabilities from yourself or from friends, you can talk your way right into poverty. So stop listening to words that say, "Honey, I don't try to save; why should I, and why should you? I'm never going to have anything anyway, and neither will you. I don't want to hear about giving to God first or any other financial stuff. Let's talk about something else." This kind of negativism will stunt your growth in prosperity. It robs God, and it robs your tin can. It will "out-fox" you financially. Read James 3:6–8 and Proverbs 18:21 to realize more fully what enormous damage your tongue can do. Then check up on yourself, watch what you say, and you will be able to help others. Whether you know it or not, God holds us accountable for everything we say.

There are two kinds of people among your working associates, friends, and family who may come into your life every day: those who make *deposits* and those who make *withdrawals*. Resist the withdrawers. They don't have anything, and they don't want you to have anything either. What can nothing tell you? Nothing of course! Because nothing doesn't know a thing.

So listen! Until you change your thinking, you will never change your financial situation. Proverbs 23:7 says, "As a man thinketh in his heart, so is he." But it is also true that "as a man listeneth, so he will be." So take heed of what you hear, for more will be given to whoever has. (See Mark 4:24.)

THINK ABOUT IT—
YOU WILL NEVER CHANGE YOUR "FINANCIAL" CONDITION UNTIL YOU CHANGE YOUR "THINKING" CONDITION.

START SMALL, SPEAK BIG

In finances, as well as in every area of life, the tongue is a powerful force that can direct the paths of our life. When I began changing my life concerning savings, I started small

Why Save?

with what I had. An inward embarrassment led me to embrace a strong will and desire to change my pitiful financial condition. So I made up my mind and started changing my thinking. And when my thinking started changing, so did my speaking—and so did my finances. I started putting a few dollars in my tin can, and as time passed, my eyes were opened to God's financial guidelines. I was a newborn baby at this, too. No one ever explained the mechanics of saving or shared the importance of financial stewardship with me. I thought I was doing just fine as a boutique proprietor. But in reality, I was a proprietor on my way to financial ruin. All that I am sharing with you in this book comes from a "been there, done that" compassionate heart.

I do believe we are living in a time during which we must learn these lessons quickly. The forces of evil directing our current government and financial institutions don't want you to learn these truths. But we have fed their coffers long enough. So don't be fooled. I'm going to share some financial information concerning their ways that will be a real eye-opener. And remember, you become accountable once you've heard the truth.

It's Time to Get in Order

So, where have you placed your tin can? To start, let me give you God's order to begin your savings plan so you can be blessed and prospered without trying to take a shortcut.

- First, pay your tithes and offerings. This is the major wealth-building foundation.
- Second, pay yourself something in your tin can. **Remember, a portion of what you earn should always be yours to keep.**
- Third, pay your bills and expenses.

Sound simple? You would think so, but not many do it.

Building Wealth Using the Tin Can Method

So let's go over these principles again.

First, pay your tithes. I know some of you are mumbling right now, saying, "By the time I get my check and pay my bills, I'm already operating in the red. How am I supposed to save anything?" Let me just say that you're operating in the red because of your misplaced order. So think about this: "Whom are you paying first?" Man, of course (your bills). Most do, and they have been doing so for many years. But that's a misplaced order. It isn't man who gives you the power to work and receive a paycheck in the first place. It is God. So God should be the one who gets paid first. The first fruits of your labor rightfully belong to Him.

Second, pay yourself (tin can) whatever you can. You're the one who worked for the money. (Note: There is no set amount. Many fail because an established amount is given as a criteria. Tin can thinking says your saving amount must be whatever you can—and then from that you graduate to more.)

Third, pay your bills.

After this, God will become your financial counselor. The sky will be the limit where He has blessed! He will increase you to finance His work on earth. And in the meantime, you will be richly blessed.

Once you begin tithing, if your "former" financial residence was located in the *county of lack*, you will need to give up or change some of your habits—such as smoking, eating out, shopping, or drinking—for a season or more. You will find some very revealing charts on this matter in chapter 10. Some of these things you will be able to pick up again. Some you should never have started in the first place, and you will want to leave them where you found them when you move.

Now, what happens to that newfound money once some of your laid-back habits are eliminated for a season or so? It goes into your tin can, which provides the initial investment in your new savings plan. As you allow God to direct you in where and what to do, it will increase. He is a God of multiplication. He desires your increase so you can continuously finance the gospel. Don't you desire to be the one who is out there blessing and giving rather than the one who is sitting around waiting for someone to bless and give to you? I know I do.

Most people rarely keep up with the money they spend on a daily basis. They often refer to their random spending as "pocket" or "chunk" change. But chunk change can add up to a hunk of change, especially if you begin to save it.

For example, let's say on Monday, at lunch time, a person goes to a fast-food restaurant and spends $4.50. Then he stops at the local convenience store for cigarettes and a snack, spending another $2.00. On Wednesday, he decides to go to another eatery and convenience store, spending another $5.00. This all adds up to a whopping $11.50 in just three days! And this same $11.50 could be going into a tin can toward their savings.

I know you may think that this is too much of a sacrifice for your small joys and luxuries. But the discipline of choosing to let these expenses start your tin can saving demonstrates your sincere desire and willingness to relocate from the *county of lack* into the *county of plenty*. This initial decision will provide a beautiful, simple beginning that will finally make you the **proud owner of a savings account!** Remember, even our president and other leaders today are telling you to save to provide and prepare for **your own personal future.**

Cigarettes are bad for your health; so are soft drinks. Fast food only puts weight on you fast. So it won't kill you to find other alternatives, such as bringing your lunch to work. Discipline yourself to do this, and you will find that you will even lose your desire for some of these things—and lose a few pounds in the process. You will also embark on another exciting adventure, one that will lead you toward a new and financially certain future—the tin can way.

Building Wealth Using the Tin Can Method

When you see your savings build as God institutes the increase stemming from your obedience, you will become as hooked on saving as you used to be on smoking, drinking, and eating. It has a magnetism that will hook you into a newfound joy of monetary accomplishment. Believe me, I know. It happened to me, and I am financially secure today because of it.

Think!

For who hath despised the day of small things?
—Zechariah 4:10

Think about this: How are tall buildings, monuments, palaces, and estates built? Did the builders say, "Abra Kadabra," and the structures appeared? No! They built them brick by brick, layer by layer, one brick at a time. When you look at skyscrapers all you see are huge, towering buildings. But they were built brick by brick, beam by beam, girder by girder. First, the foundation was laid. Then, after a period of time, the work of construction made it appear. It progressively exploded into a massive giant, just as your funds will, little by little, until you will need to trade your tin can in on a barrel.

Despising small beginnings will hinder your progress even when you take a job. If you come in at the bottom and anxiously desire to be at the top, you will stay at the bottom. Why? You have to prove yourself. As you are diligent, your work performance increases, and good habits are developed (which are considered every day), in most cases, promotion takes place. The same is true of finances. Before you know it, accumulation takes place.

Trade With What You Have—Save With What You Have

Remember the three servants in the Bible who were each

WHY SAVE?

given talents. The first one received five talents; the second, two; and the third, one. Each was entrusted to a stewardship from their master over the measure they received. They were to utilize what they had been entrusted with to the best of their abilities to produce more.

As this teaching in Matthew 25 states, the one with the one talent didn't do what he should have done to add to his one talent. When the master returned, he was rebuked. He wasn't a good steward over that one talent. He hid (hoarded) it. We'll look at hoarding in chapter 2. So the master of this hoarding servant took the talent away from him and gave it to the one who had five. The steward with the five talents had proven himself to be more prudent, consistent, diligent, and obedient. And the same was true of the servant who received two.

As Jesus taught, if you will be a good steward over little, He will make you ruler over much (Matt. 25:21). But the trouble is, many don't even have a little to be a good steward over because they've squandered it away foolishly. Most reside in the county of economic lack without any hope of moving. And in the case of many, if they do have a little, they don't respect it as being significant. So the doors for many are often closed because of poor stewardship over the little God has entrusted to their care.

We often pray, "I'll start a savings account when I get $5,000. God, please bless me with $5,000 to start the account." Or, "God, if I could just save $25,000 dollars...." The fact of the matter is, you can have $25,000. But most haven't saved it because they haven't even tried. I know, because I was one of them.

So keep thinking, always thinking! The problem with thinking that you have to have a lot of money to start saving is that the amount never seems to manifest itself at *one* time. Satan makes sure of it and discourages them from starting. So they don't start. They just idle the months and years away hoping, never coming to the realization that the huge amount isn't coming. They don't put on their thinking cap to employ another method to make it happen.

In an issue of the *New Age Journal* I came across an interesting article about the *The Tightwad Gazette,* a newsletter that promoted frugality in which an article appeared that inspired me tremendously. It was written by a woman named Amy Dacyzyn, who along with her husband and six children managed to save $49,000 in seven years, on an income of less than $30,000 a year. They spent another $38,000 on "investment purchases," the article said, such as furniture and vehicles.

Now I don't know all the ins and outs of their success, but I mention her story to substantiate that it doesn't—contrary to the beliefs of many—require a gigantic salary to save. What it does require is obedience in following God's economic blueprint and discipline.

How many times have we found ourselves begging and hoping that God would send a financial blessing our way? You don't have to beg Him. God wants all of His children to be blessed. It doesn't glorify God if we aren't. He promises, "Beloved, I wish above all things that thou mayest prosper and be in health, even as your soul prospereth" (3 John 2). But for God to desire your prosperity isn't enough. You must desire it enough to implement His plan to make it a reality. That's why the Word says that "thou mayest" prosper. One may—or may not—depending upon one's desire. It's your choice!

LOOK AROUND YOU DAILY TO FIND GOD'S BLESSINGS

We must learn to let God's Word be true and every man a liar. Why? Because our blessings are connected to the covenant that God made with Abraham, which says his seed would be blessed.

"So why don't we see it?" you ask. "Isn't He the same God?" Yes, He is! He hasn't changed. Most can't see His blessing because Christians and non-Christians alike are looking for blessings to come in the way they want them to come. Remember, God's ways are not our ways, and neither are His thoughts our thoughts (Isa. 55:8–9). Yet in another verse He promises to answer before you call (Isa. 65:24).

So where are these blessings then? In the things He gives us every day. They are in our next breath, in our jobs, in our homes, and yes, in our paychecks. But because many aren't good stewards over the little they have, they fail to see these things, and they throw them away as used-up tin. And this, in turn, causes God to pass over the "unthinking" when making others ruler over much.

How many of you have asked God to rain upon you $50,000 or some other great monetary windfall? Now that you have started to think, what would you say if His response was, "I will give it to you, but not in a lump sum. It will come in small increments that will total that amount." Would you be upset knowing that He was going to give it to you in that manner? Would you say, "God, since You can't give it to me all at once, I don't want it?"

Of course, it's always wonderful to have or receive abundance all at once. But if you don't have anything, if someone is willing to give it to you brick by brick, shouldn't you take it anyway? Yes, you should! And you should say, "God, I'll take it any way you choose to give it to me," and allow Him to bless you!

Think again. Let's suppose you asked the Lord for that same amount, and He told you, "Okay, I'll give it to you, but I don't have any large bills. All I have are one dollar bills. But I will give it to you over a period of time until it totals the desired amount." Would you complain? Would you still say, "No, if I can't have it all at once, I don't want it at all!" Of course you wouldn't! At least I hope that's what you would say. These examples represent the start small principles behind tin can saving.

Building Wealth Using the Tin Can Method

> **Think About It—**
> God answers prayers and has given you that $50,000 you don't see in front of you right now. You just haven't seen it because you despise small beginnings.

If you're undisciplined and don't keep a record of your earnings and spending, you will never see even half of what you make. And you won't be saving because you're not thinking. So put your financial thinking cap on, and keep it on! In the coming chapters I'm going to challenge you in those areas where you have shown financial discipline over the years while at the same time neglecting savings. You didn't think you could keep a steady schedule of savings, so you just started and stopped all the time. Yet, there have been no late payments made on your car note for the last three to five years. You have been faithful to make your interest payments on all your credit cards. And your house payments have been consistent over the years.

If you can be disciplined in these matters, why can't you start doing this in the area of savings? Your savings deserve to be included and treated in the same manner as your other financial obligations. Even more so when you begin to . . .

> **Think About It—**
> Because saving pertains more to your welfare than some of these other things mentioned.

Once you start, little by little as you make it a bill to yourself, it will become such a part of you that you won't be able to remember when it wasn't. And, you will never find yourself without funds or lacking.

Why Save?

- To leave an inheritance to your children's children, enabling them to continually enhance and finance the gospel.
- To be prepared financially for the "good deals" God will bring before His obedient servants as the wealthier wicked begin to transfer their wealth into the hands of the obedient just.
- To lend and never have to borrow.
- To be God's light in a world of darkness, leading those who are in darkness into His marvelous light.
- To be a blessing wherever and whenever you go in and out.

Paying tithes and offerings are the necessary compound ingredients that make our tin can savings complete and beneficial. In the following pages you will learn that starting small in savings is necessary if one is to improve his or her financial condition. And you will also learn—security is just around the bend.

Now let's move on to chapter 2 and get you enrolled in God's Financial Academy of accountability.

Two
God's Financial Academy

It's time to get enrolled in **God's Financial Academy!** It has existed for thousands of years, and its sound financial principles have prospered many students. We've all heard of the great wealth and prosperity of one of its **first** and best-known students—Father Abraham.

This school's curriculum has never changed; its classrooms are never filled to capacity. Each student who implements the academy's financial plans is guaranteed phenomenal success. No one who has properly applied its rules has been disappointed. This academy boasts of the 100 percent success record of its graduates. And there are no qualifications for enrollment—its application simply states, "Whosoever will may come"—*it's free!*

Accountability

Accountability is the primary and foremost subject on the class schedule in God's Financial Academy. May the Holy Spirit embed these primary truths deep into your spirit.

Are we our brother's keeper? Have we not, by God's written Word, been given a mandate to train up our children in the way they should go so they may survive when

GOD'S FINANCIAL ACADEMY

thrust into the world? Should we not then also assist in holding one another up to prevent a further declining of moral values and standards? God's academy answers these questions with a resounding *yes*.

You see, the fall of one will most assuredly affect others. *Accountability*—sharing God's concern for the welfare of others and holding ourselves accountable to His Word—is a very important biblical key.

For example, if your neighbor's crop should become infested with locusts, wouldn't you want to assist him in destroying them in order to prevent the destruction of your crop? To say it is your neighbor's problem only is to say your crop is immune, but destroyers are no respecters of persons. Your crop will begin to look rather appetizing after they have devoured your neighbor's crop. Assisting your neighbor in destroying the locusts from his crop secures yours from contamination.

Accountability stands up and demands to be respected. One stands a far better chance of being heard in a matter when supported by others. No man is an island. We all need one another and should be accountable to each other concerning our actions.

ONE BAD APPLE *CAN* SPOIL THE WHOLE BUNCH

We've all heard the saying, "One bad apple can spoil the bunch." From one bad apple, infestation begins to take place, and the spreading of contamination takes root. The key is to get rid of the contamination before it spoils the bunch, rotting every apple.

Association can bring assimilation—be it positive or negative. This is true in financial matters as well. The Word states: "What communion hath light with darkness...Come out from among them and be ye separate, says the Lord" (2 Cor. 6:14, 17). This is a universal spiritual law. It most definitely applies to our financial matters.

Building Wealth Using the Tin Can Method

Accountability in Tithes and Offerings

There is an area of our finances where this principle of assimilation is most profound. And I want to make the following profoundly impactful statement: *We must come out from associating with people who don't pay their tithes and offerings!* Remember—all that God's written Word says is true. Whether one heeds it or not is certainly up to the individual, but this doesn't nullify the truth. So continue reading, and allow me to expound a bit more on this subject before you label me *crazy!*

Maybe you're wondering why I didn't just say it this way: **You have no business associating with anyone who is not paying his or her tithes and offerings.** In this instance, the word *associating* means "spending an enormous amount of quality time with another." Casual conversation isn't regarded as quality time. This is not to say that you are better than another. What I am saying is this: *You are who you hang out with.* It is as Paul says, "Do not be deceived: Evil company corrupts good habits" (1 Cor. 15:33, NKJV).

We all need to become more serious about life and what God says about it. Time is short! God's Word states that He came to give us life—more abundant life. But to receive that abundant life we must implement whatever is required to receive the benefits. Yes, this is truth, there are prerequisites. But the choice lies with us. We have the choice to choose this day whom and what we will serve.

Because we should be our brother's keeper, we should devote time in sharing from Scripture, God's written Word, about tithes and offerings. We should tell those we know about the benefits their households would receive for being obedient. And of course, we must *always* devote our time and effort toward winning souls.

But to go beyond this duty would require our investing too much valuable time in *stiff-necked, disobedient, "going-nowhere" people.* They may not induce negative results for you today, but their negative influence may show up on the scene tomorrow. This may be something you have never heard before. The message I'm writing now is what I believe He has given me concerning this topic. There are scriptures and examples in the Word that confirm what I'm saying. I didn't establish the law or write the Word of God, but I can tell you that the positive benefits for obeying God's Word are magnificent! You can talk to God personally for yourself about what His written Word says.

ACCOUNTABILITY IN UNEQUALLY YOKED MARRIAGES

There are many unequally yoked marriages in which one mate is a nonbeliever. This produces a real problem with accountability. In order to apply God's Financial Academy rules to this situation, if you fit into this category, hopefully at least *one* of you is paying tithes and offerings. For a certainty, one obedient spouse is better than none in a household. God is understanding, loving, and full of mercy, and He will bless and even prosper the obedient spouse to some degree in an unequally yoked marriage—with the disobedient spouse reaping some of the blessings. But the *full, complete scope and magnitude of blessing and prosperity* will never be experienced because the two aren't living in one accord concerning God's Word on tithes and offerings. When one is in unbelief, it will affect the other.

Even though many times we think we are doing well, we may still be living **far** beneath our privileges because of disobedience. We would be astounded if God should choose to allow us to glimpse in the Spirit what we *could* or *should* have been experiencing if we had heeded His words in total obedience. You see, how can two walk together harmoniously unless they both agree? (See Amos 3:3.) The Word says that one can chase a thousand and two can put ten thousand to flight (Deut. 32:30). There is greater power in numbers, be it positive or negative.

BUILDING WEALTH USING THE TIN CAN METHOD

A spouse who doesn't pay tithes and offerings could influence his or her obedient mate to waver and possibly even stop obeying God during an adverse financial crisis. This would bring about more financial devastation. Avoid negative thoughts like the following: *Maybe my spouse is right about paying tithes and offerings. Maybe we could get caught up on some of our bills if I quit paying them for a month or so.* With such thoughts Satan could bring more havoc into the household.

The power of thought is a powerful thing, especially if it's acted upon. This is why it's easier for two to walk together in harmony when they are in agreement. When adverse times come upon the scene (and they will as long as Satan is alive), each can uphold the other in encouragement and faith. They both can travel the same path without sideswiping each other.

Therefore, in the case of an unequally yoked marriage, the obedient one would do well to be on his or her face before the Lord in prayer and fasting. This could break the curse of disobedience over the other, bringing them into submission to God's Word.

Children under the age of accountability will receive blessings that stem from your actions as their parents. You are commanded by the Word of God to teach and train your children in the way that they should go. Then as they mature and reach the age of accountability, they won't depart from those teachings (Prov. 22:6). They will pass God's wisdom on to the next generation. I suggest strongly that you train them to tithe early so they won't become as stiff-necked as many are today, making it more difficult to train them once they become young adults.

If you have friends and other family members who haven't heard the principles of God's Word, use this as a ministry opportunity to share the gospel—as well as God's financial truths with them. Show them Scripture references concerning the rendering of the first fruits of one's labor unto God. Ask the Holy Spirit to assist and direct you. Then let them know that once they've heard the Word, they will be held accountable to it.

Now, for the 80 percent of church-going nontithers who have heard and are familiar with God's Word on tithing, there is **no** excuse for their disobedience in this area. This group, be they friend, family, or foe, should certainly be steered clear of as far as constant and serious association is concerned. They will not reach their maximum financial potential even though they may appear to have done so. And they will hinder you from reaching yours.

Many curses hover over peoples' lives because of their ignorance and disobedience in this area. God's Word states in Malachi 3:9 that nontithers are cursed with a curse as a result of robbing God of tithes and offerings. This group isn't only defrauding themselves of riches, but they will hinder you as well. This demonstrates the principle of association leading to assimilation.

THE ACHAN PRINCIPLE

A strong biblical example to support this position of separation can be found in the account of the children of Israel's victorious battle over Jericho and their subsequent defeat at Ai.

Israel's victory over Jericho was mysterious and supernatural. But it was Joshua's obedience in leadership that really led to their victory. God had already instructed Joshua concerning what He would do for the children of Israel if they would hearken unto Him. Joshua was promised prosperity and good success if he would be "strong and courageous, observing the law and all that is written therein" (Josh. 1:8). In other words, God told Joshua, "Just be obedient."

We can see in Joshua 1:2–9 that Joshua honored God by being obedient. His obedience caused the children of Israel to capture Jericho. God has always remained true to His Word. All of Israel remained in one accord as they followed

Building Wealth Using the Tin Can Method

God's instructions given to Joshua, and victory was secured. You see, once Joshua was given instructions by God concerning the method he should use for this battle, Joshua became accountable (liable, responsible, or answerable) to God's instructions. To disobey would mean defeat, and Joshua would be responsible because he was their leader.

So Jericho was a victory. But the next test and battle came at the little city of Ai. This was a much smaller city than the fortified Jericho. But because of its strategic location, it had to be taken.

Joshua's first attempt to defeat Ai failed. Joshua and his men had just defeated the huge city of Jericho, destroying the enormous fortified walls that surrounded it. Yet they couldn't even take a small city like Ai with no protective walls!

Joshua thought he had followed God's instructions, but thirty-six of Joshua's men were killed by the enemy forces. This defeat caused Joshua to seek God again for clarity in the situation (Josh. 7:5). *Why had God allowed this?* Joshua couldn't understand what was happening. But as he sought God for clarity and insight, God revealed to him that there was *sin in the camp.* Someone had disobeyed, taking for himself some of the accursed things under the ban. As as evangelist once said, "It doesn't take but one to take you up and only one to take you down!" Not many—just one! And so it is in your household and in any *wrong associations*.

Joshua sought the Lord for a method to pinpoint the culprit. God had declared in Joshua 7:12, **"Neither will I be with you anymore except ye destroy the accursed from among you."** You see, God may not move or work miracles under unclean conditions or surroundings. **This could be a reason why more miracles are not being displayed individually and collectively today in the church.** The answer could be that too many accursed or out-of-order disobedient ones are in our midst.

God isn't obligated to do anything for anyone who is acting contrary to His Word. We must obey in order for Him to produce more miracles on our behalf. This is exactly what He was saying to Joshua: "Thou cannot stand before thine enemies, until you take away the accused thing from among you" (Josh. 7:13).

God was seeking confession of sins, repentance, and restoration to fellowship. God deals severely with sin because sin is always severe. The punishment in this case? "He that is taken with the accursed thing shall be burnt with fire, he and all that he hath" (Josh. 7:15).

Joshua now had the unpleasant but necessary task of exposing and eliminating the violator's family. He discovered that Achan of the tribe of Judah was the one who took the accursed thing. Achan's solo act troubled and affected everyone, causing even the innocent to suffer. The entire family of Israel was polluted and affected by the offense of Achan. None of the others had anything to do with what Achan was doing. Yet they suffered. Thirty-six of them forfeited their lives. Remember, *disobedience will cause chaos.*

Achan's entire immediate family suffered from his act. Corporate punishment was inflicted upon all in his family because of the sin of one. Joshua said, "Why hast thou troubled us? The Lord shall trouble thee this day. And all Israel stoned him with stones and burned them (his family) with fire after they had stoned them with stones" (Josh. 7:25).

JOASH AND JEHOIDA

Another example of the biblical principle of assimilation can be found in 2 Chronicles 24. King Joash was doing fine while he walked in the ways of the Lord. The priest Jehoida was wise in the wisdom and knowledge of God and served King Joash well. Then Jehoida died. Allow me to say here that it is so important to seek wise counsel from God-fearing, obedient advisors and friends who are spiritually competent to advise you. Remember, it takes only one to take you up and only one to bring you down. And Joash's actions took the whole nation down!

After Jehoiada died, Joash allowed the princes of Judah to influence and guide him in wrong ways. He listened to them rather than seeking God. He led the nation to leave the house of the Lord and worship idols, bringing the wrath of God upon all of Judah—not just on Joash and his foolish advisors in Jerusalem. God gave Judah many chances to return to Him—but they chose not to heed. In 2 Chronicles 24:20 He told them, "Why do you transgress the commandments of the Lord? You *cannot prosper.*"

This is still the Word of the Lord! Disobedience will cause all who are influenced to not prosper. So get in order! Repent and change your ways concerning your finances. Don't let disobedience cause more heartache, suffering, and death as it did for King Joash. Pay your tithes and offerings no matter how little you make. And pay yourself. Then watch God fight your financial battles and work miracles. God's hands are not short, and His abilities are not limited.

Adam, Eve's Accountability Failure

Today every man and woman alive is reaping humongous negative consequences because of the disobedience of Adam and Eve. The apostle Paul regarded the Corinthian church as polluted because of the presence of *one* single offender (1 Cor. 5). The specific sin at issue had been pinpointed in them—but they refused to deal with it. A man (brother in Christ) was having an affair with his stepmother, and the members of the church decided to ignore the situation. The apostle Paul insisted profoundly that they had a responsibility to uphold standards of morality found in the Word of God. To ignore the situation would have allowed that one member to jeopardize the spiritual health of all.

We see this principle at work from the very beginning. Eve's one disobedient act caused a curse for *all* of mankind. What could life have been if she had been obedient? What could life have been if Adam had resisted, refusing to partner with her in disobedience?

DAVID AND BATHSHEBA

In the case of David and his sin with Bathsheba, Bathsheba's innocent husband, Uriah, died because of their offense (2 Sam. 11). Many times death occurs as a result of disobedience. Death in our finances is no different. That too stems from disobedience.

One disobedient Achan today in your family or among your associates may produce similar results. You may even know someone who has died because of whom that person associated with. Many people have even suffered the consequences meant for someone else—all because of association. **There is no such thing as a private sin.**

All sin affects others. Many laws have been enacted because of someone's decision to make a change. Because of the act on one persistent atheist woman, Madalyn Murray O'Hair, prayer was taken out of the classroom in America—affecting our youth and entire nation *negatively*.

Remember that the personal sin of each believer will affect the church at large. Sin involves society, and we comprise society—therefore accountability, being our brother's keeper, demands attention.

> **THINK ABOUT IT—**
> A LACK OF ACCOUNTABILITY HAS PRODUCED THE ILL FINANCIAL AND MORAL CONDITIONS IN WHICH WE ARE PRESENTLY LIVING. THE LONGER WE WITHHOLD A DEMAND FOR ACCOUNTABILITY, THE LARGER BECOMES THE EFFECTS OF THE CURSE. SO IT IS WITH US AS INDIVIDUALS.

So again, I repeat—we would do well not to associate

with nontithers. **It is detrimental to one's health and wealth.**

I believe the giving of corporate tithes and offerings in the church would produce miracles that would be beyond the belief of its members. Churches who think they're doing well would realize how far they register below the level of God's desired blessings and prosperity. Churches would need to literally open banks overnight, and they would buy or build major hotels and restaurants, amazing the world. Then the scripture in Deuteronomy 28:12, which says, "You will lend and never borrow, you will be the head and not the tail," would manifest before our eyes.

The magnitude of the revelation of Malachi 3:11 would appear: "I will open up the windows of heaven and pour out a blessing that there shall not be room enough to receive." Churches would be pleading with people to share in their overflow of abundance. This is not an impossibility. It only requires obedience. And I am praying to see this come to pass!

THE OBEDIENT 20 PERCENT

Have you ever thought about the 20 percent group of obedient servants who are tithing, paying offerings, and taking upon themselves all the church responsibilities of spreading of the gospel? The church is where it is today financially because of the grace of God at work through this group.

Think how much more successful the church could be if more members ceased stealing God's money and more churches dealt with the flagrant sin of non-tithing among its members.

We must truly be serious to bridge this gap.

"We are serious," you say.

Okay, if you are truly serious, next time you're in the house of God, check with the person sitting next to you and kindly ask, "Pardon me, sir or ma'am. I'm very serious about my financial matters, as is God. I am paying tithes and offerings. I don't desire to rob God anymore. Are you a tither? Do you understand God's order concerning tithes and offerings? If not, I would be happy to share with you what God's Word has to say about it. If you are already familiar with it and are simply desiring not to obey, I do pray you will reconsider. But until then, I must sit elsewhere so as not to worship with an accursed and disobedient person. I'll pray for God's wisdom to mature in your life. Now if you would, please excuse me."

Could we be serious and bold enough in regard to the things of God do this? Father Abraham obeyed God and separated himself from his family. God told him to "get thee out of thy country, from thy kindred and from thy father's house into a land that I will shew thee." In other words, "Get away from them—far away." (See Genesis 12:1.) I'm sure this was a hard decision for Abraham. But Abraham feared God more than he feared his family. Abraham knew well that obedience is better than sacrifice. And what happened? Abraham prospered beyond belief!

God will always award handsomely for obedience. Could you be bold, brave, and obedient as Abraham and get up and walk away?

You're probably thinking right now that you wouldn't want to hurt another's feelings. But we care more about man's feelings than we do about God's Word, God's feelings, and God's blessings. He is the one who created us in the first place. Without Him, we wouldn't exist. A curse doesn't care about your feelings, and neither does the devil. Satan prefers your being disobedient so as to detain your present and future blessings, along with those of your family. And if your disobedient associates really cared about you, they would get in order to avoid letting their negative talk and disobedience affect your financial well-being.

Exposure many times can be a very successful means of inducing accountability. **Millions of church goers have**

heard the gospel for far too long to remain a part of the 20/80 ratio of nontithers. How long should they continue attending church, robbing God, you, me, and others of our supernatural blessings and prosperity? Enough is enough! They must be told that they are loved too much to be allowed to continue to remain in their sin.

> How terrible that you should boast about your spirituality and yet you let this sort of thing go on. Don't you realize that if even *one* person is allowed to go on sinning, soon all will be affected? Remove this wicked person from among you so that you can stay pure.
> —1 CORINTHIANS 5:6–7, NLT, ITALICS ADDED

ACCOUNTABLE LOVE MUST BE TOUGH

I recall an excellent book on accountability in relationships entitled *Love Must Be Tough,* which was written by well-known Christian author James Dobson. It would do well for you to read it. Dr. Dobson talks about adultery and how the spouse who has been betrayed must be tough in giving his or her unfaithful mate an alternative—either repent and straighten up, or leave. The author teaches that the adulterer must be held accountable for his or her sin. When the obedient one allows the violator to remain, and continually accepts that person's wrongdoing, it only allows the situation to worsen.

We can't continue to do wrong and expect to reap blessings from our wrongdoing. God won't allow such a thing. Just because you didn't pay today doesn't mean you won't pay tomorrow. God will not allow disobedience to run rampant in His church without exacting the price for it. There is a cost. Paul makes this point clear:

> When I wrote to you before, I told you not to associate with people who indulge in sexual sin. But I wasn't

talking about unbelievers who indulge in sexual sin, or who are greedy or are swindlers or idol worshipers. You would have to leave this world to avoid people like that. What I meant was that you are not to associate with anyone who claims to be a Christian yet indulges in sexual sin, or is greedy, or worships idols, or is abusive, or a drunkard, or a swindler. Don't even eat with such people. It isn't my responsibility to judge outsiders, but it certainly is your job to judge those inside the church who are sinning in these ways. God will judge those on the outside; but as the Scriptures say, "You must remove the evil person from *among you*."

—1 Corinthians 5:9–13, NLT, italics added

We must love one another enough, as God has so commanded, not to allow disobedience to run rampant. This is why we have laws. Sin and its evil fruit must always be dealt with.

It's unpleasant to discipline our children when they're disobedient, yet it is very necessary to keep them from going further astray. Your financial matters are so important that they could be a link to your destiny and to your children's children's destinies. That alone should be enough to demand accountability from one another.

The problems of financial accountability are a major cause of marital strife. According to statistics, approximately 50 percent of all marriages fail. Eighty percent of divorced couples between the ages of twenty and thirty say that financial problems were the primary cause of their divorce. If statistics would be taken concerning these couples in the area of tithes and offerings, I believe we would find that the majority of them **have not** been obedient in this area. Their disregard for God's Word in this area has allowed the curse of divorce to penetrate their lives.

Building Wealth Using the Tin Can Method

A Call for Tougher Love

There is a need for the church to become tougher in the area of tithes and offerings. To truly succeed, the rules of God's Financial Academy must be applied.

Church growth can be stunted because of disobedient members. A tithe is a tenth, and an offering is beyond that. Even if one gives $5,000 in tithes, if he should be giving $10,000, then according to Malachi 3:8–10, he is a robber and disobedient. God sees and knows all—and He can certainly count! You may fool man, but you can't fool God. Malachi 3:16 says that He keeps a supernatural and accurate record of all our deeds:

> Then they that feared the Lord spake often one to another: and the Lord hearkened, and heard it, and a *book of remembrance* was written before him for them that feared the Lord, and that thought upon his name.

Which would be better? Two thousand obedient tithe-and-offering-paying members or ten thousand disobedient members?

Many leaders are "hung up" on having a huge edifice and ministry coupled with a large congregation. **But great numbers do not equal great effectiveness.** Obedience cannot exist harmoniously with disobedience. Many churches are filled with fussing and nonagreement—and this stagnates potential growth.

Remember—light and darkness cannot agree. The church must address the problem of disobedience as Joshua did. God held him accountable to discover and deal with the disobedience before he could go on to win other victories. Had he not dealt with Achan's sin, all Israel would have suffered, and more obedient soldiers would have lost their lives.

ANANIAS AND SAPPHIRA

Let's look at another account of disobedience. The disobedience of Ananias and Sapphira cost them their lives (Acts 5). By now you're probably thinking, *Wow! There's sure a lot of dying going on around here. This accountability issue is nothing to play with.* How smart you are—it's not! Sapphira could have been spared if she had chosen not to side with her husband and walk down the same path. She had an individual choice to do otherwise, as we all do. So making the right choice is vital.

Remember, one obedient person in a household is better than none. If Sapphira had chosen obedience, she would have been a widow, yes, but she would have been alive. She certainly could have remarried. But she chose the route of her husband and received the same fate. When asked about how much money they had sold their property for, both lied to the Holy Spirit. They were two peas in a pod, and they both died for their actions.

Sapphira acted just like Adam who, although he knew that Eve was doing wrong, didn't hold her accountable, and walked down the same road of deception and disobedience. The association of one with the other produced negative results for both of them—and us. All men inherit spiritual (separation from God) and physical death because of Adam and Eve's sin.

Disobedience in paying ones tithes and offerings is detrimental to one's health and wealth. It is dangerous—and deadly—to be connected or associated with out-of-order, disobedient people.

Why do lions hang out with lions, chickens with chickens, foxes with foxes, alcoholics with alcoholics, and drug users with drug users? It's because they all share a common goal or bond with each other. What do you suppose would happen if a chicken hung out with a fox, or a deer with a lion? Dinner, that's what. One of them would end up an entrée. Why? Disorder. This is what produces death.

The growth of many churches have been stunted and robbed of reaching the goals God intended for them because of the evil, ugly spirit of disobedience. It is pure sorcery and witchcraft! Jealousy, envy, division, adultery, prideful position seekers, fornication, hindrance of spiritual gifts, procrastination and laziness, poverty and lack (big time), businesses not coming forth, prosperity resistance, strife, contention, and a spirit of hatred and prejudice are all results of disobedience. This is what you get when the church is divided. And the list could go on.

No wonder it's so hard for many churches. These aren't the best of conditions in which to do the work of the gospel. No wonder it's so difficult to get the body to come together in one accord on anything. There is havoc in the house! And the "accursed thing or people" must be discovered and dealt with.

Let me also say this: I say uncompromisingly, if you are under any ministry and the pastor as well as the leadership aren't paying their tithes and offerings, **Leave! Run!** Yes, run as fast as you can, leaving a trail of smoke behind you. No matter how many prayers they pray with, for, or over you, they will be useless. If the head is out of order, surely every one under their leadership will suffer somehow. Don't allow anyone who isn't paying their tithes and offerings to pray for your financial prosperity. God won't hear their prayer! How can they believe for your prosperity when their own is cursed? That is ludicrous!

THINK ABOUT IT—
A "GOOD" THING IS VASTLY DIFFERENT FROM A "GOD" THING. ACCOUNTABILITY IS CALLING! WILL YOU HEED ITS CALL?

Now let me talk to you nontithers. That you are reading

this material from God's Financial Academy shows there is much hope!

If you have come into the knowledge and realization that there *is* a God...if you have been saved...obeying and respecting what He says is very important.

Your disobedience in the area of tithing is costing you and your family the portion of wealth that is rightfully yours as a joint heir with Christ Jesus. Jesus bought you for a price with His life so you could be blessed in the New Covenant's wonderful promises and provisions. But disobedience summons the devourer. And it is the devourer who will destroy any accumulation of funds.

Why would anyone fail to claim funds that have been accumulated for them? If it takes obedience to receive access to what is rightfully yours, then obedient you ought to be.

If you're suffering financially, you have no one to blame but yourself. You are holding the key that will unlock your treasure box. If you're an Achan who isn't making payment of your tithes and offerings, instead spending God's money for your own wants, such disobedience is costing you a hefty sum. It is costing you your share of great wealth. It may even be costing you the solution to your many problems. Ecclesiastes 10:19 says that "money answereth all things." Your disobedience is hindering you. So beware, nontither. Repent, and God will bless.

IN GOD WE TRUST?

The whole matter of holding ourselves and others accountable has to do with the matter of trust. Do we really trust in God in our local church? Or are we merely giving lip service and playing church? One of God's basic academy rules is this: Trust and obey; be accountable to His will.

I recall years ago when the main necessities of living—housing, food, and utilities—were at a minimum. Americans had conditioned themselves to give top priority to these things. Even though salaries and wages were much lower then, saving money was more respected and honored. Giving to God was also more important. Money didn't seem to flow as freely, and every penny was carefully spent to insure survival. After all, not too much of anything else could be squeezed out of a person's income. *Or could it?*

Then modernizations such as telephones, televisions, credit cards, and computers began to spring up. And somehow all of these new niceties were squeezed out of that **same** salary.

In the rush to modernize, however, less attention was given to issues of tithes, offerings, giving, and savings. These most important priorities were minimized until today they have taken a back seat in many lives. Most people can continuously condition themselves to pay rent, cable fees, car notes, insurance, and other bills, yet seldom make the same commitment to include tithes, offerings, and paying themselves in savings.

This is why I believe that, according to God, this entire nation is a thief (Mal. 3:9). A lot of money is being deducted from employee's pay checks to pay for things one never sees. In some instances, it's mandatory that certain deductions for charities be taken out of one's salary, whether they want to contribute or not.

Business-Deducted Tithes?

My sister, niece, and I once discussed an issue that had come before the government employees in my hometown. It involved the government's request that every city employee own a computer. The reason given was that employees would be able to do a better job at home through the use of these computers. A proposal was submitted and voted upon by the city board, making low-interest loans available to government employees to purchase a computer. The money loaned to an employee for the purchase of the computer would be deducted from the employee's check via payroll deduction. How convenient!

I'm sure many will participate in this lucrative venture *if* it is approved. But whether it gets approved or not, here's the point I'm trying to make. Around this nation, many senseless deductions of various kinds are being deducted *by permission,* I assume, to pay for a number of different things employees would otherwise say they couldn't afford.

Wouldn't it be a tremendous national honor for God if employees nationwide permitted 10 percent or more of their salaries to be deducted for tithes and offerings?

You may think I'm crazy again for talking like this. You may even feel like putting the book down because it goes against your present way of thinking. But, don't put the book down. Keep reading and open your mind to receive wisdom. Someone has to say this, and someone needs to hear it.

Why would you regard man and disregard God? God could allow your jobs to be snatched from under you in a blink of an eye. You might even find yourself "flat broke." God's Word says that it is God who gives you the power to get wealth—not you yourself. If you permit these companies to take money out for everything else, why can't you permit them to take money out for this cause? God's Word substantiates it.

> O nations of the world, recognize the Lord. Recognize that the Lord is glorious and strong. Give to the Lord the glory He deserves! *Bring your offering and come to worship Him.*
> —1 CHRONICLES 16:28–29, NLT, ITALICS ADDED

This nation's money reads, "In God we trust." *But do we really trust Him?* Do you trust Him enough to give back to Him the portion He requires out of honor and respect? Our

BUILDING WEALTH USING THE TIN CAN METHOD

money says "we"—but do we as a people? For most, everyone and everything gets a percentage of their money except God. We must all trust God and stop speaking with a forked tongue.

Can you imagine the blessings that would fall upon this nation if we would all do what was honorable in the sight of God—first? If for no other reason than to reverence and respect His Word, I assure you, we would be blessed beyond measure! The eternal financial security of ourselves and of our children would be locked in for sure. Our heavenly Father would be well pleased, and everyone would benefit.

God says in Malachi 3 that Israel had robbed Him, even the whole nation, and that they were cursed with a curse. I personally believe this scripture could be applied to America today. If 10 percent of income were to be deducted from every American's paycheck to avoid this curse, "we the people" would certainly speak up, saying, "You can't take *my* money and give 10 percent to God. That's *my* money!" Yet many flush more than 10 percent down the drain in bingo, smoking, telephone bills, gambling, drinking, and other things (which we will also cover in a coming chapter). They say nothing while banks, the government, and other foreign entities make various deductions from their paychecks.

America needs to realize that giving 10 percent to God would *secure* our welfare. We are a people who are out of order in this nation. Our priorities are out of sync. God's judgment will come upon the wicked, and His blessings of prosperity and superabundance will come upon the obedient. Which group will you be in?

To help you decide, memorize and become familiar with the following Scriptures:

> Will a man rob God? Yet ye have robbed me. But ye say, wherein have we robbed thee? In tithes and offer-

ings. Ye are cursed with a curse: for ye have robbed me, even this *whole nation.*

Bring ye all the tithes into the storehouse, that there may be meat in mine house, and prove me now herewith, saith the Lord of host, if I will not open you the windows of heaven, and pour you out a blessing, that there shall not be room enough to receive it. And I will rebuke the devourer for your sakes, and he shall not destroy the fruits of your ground: neither shall your vine cast her fruit before the time in the field, saith the Lord of hosts. And all nations shall call you blessed: for ye shall be a delight some land, saith the Lord of hosts.

Your words have been stout against me, saith the Lord. Yet ye say, what have we spoken so much against thee? Ye have said, It is vain to serve God: and what profit is it that we have kept his ordinance, and that we have walked mournfully before the Lord of hosts? And now we call the proud happy; yea, they that work wickedness are set up; yea they that tempt God are even delivered.

Then they that feared the Lord spake often one to another: and the Lord hearkened, and heard it, *and a book of remembrance was written before him for them that feared the Lord,* and that thought upon his name. And they shall be mine, saith the Lord of hosts, in that day when I make up my jewels; and I will spare them, as a man spareth his own son that serveth him. Then shall ye return, and discern between the righteous and the wicked, between him that serveth God and him that serveth him not.
—Malachi 3:8–18, italics added

For behold, the day cometh, that shall burn a an oven; and all the proud, yea, and all that do wickedly, shall be stubble: and the day that cometh shall burn them up, saith the Lord of hosts, that it shall leave them neither

root nor branch. But unto you that fear my name shall the sun of righteousness arise with healing in his wings; and ye shall go forth, and grow up as calves of the stall. And ye shall tread down the wicked; for they shall be ashes under the soles of your feet in the day that I shall do this, saith the Lord of hosts. SELAH.
—MALACHI 4:1–3

A WORD TO OUR ILLUSTRIOUS SENIOR CITIZENS— DUES ARE NOT THE SAME AS TITHES AND OFFERINGS

Before we close this brief presentation of God's Financial Academy's rules of accountability, I need to say something to our senior Christians and non-Christians about the tradition of *dues*. Many Christian seniors look to God to take care of them through His deep compassion. And they are dearly comforted in His love knowing they are not being allowed to compete in a world that is harsh and uncaring toward senior citizens. Many feel that Social Security is adequately doing the job of taking care of them. If not Social Security, they look to some other program or to their loved ones.

The term *dues* refers to what many older folk have referred to as money to be given to their church. But God's rules and laws mean what they say and say what they mean—no one is exempt. From my understanding, many refer to dues as a portion they have set aside or plan to give God. But this doesn't qualify as a tithe. Let's take a look at this popular position in light of what Scripture says.

Nowhere in the Word of God will you find anything that in any way insinuates that dues from any elderly person, even if they are old and sweet, will reap the same benefits as tithes and offerings. *First fruits are not dues.* First fruits are tithes. Remember, a tithe is a tenth. Now if some have been referring to dues as tithes, and their dues equal what their tithes should be, then they are tithes. Maybe it was simply easier for some to understand the term *dues* over *tithes,* and of course God will know this and honor it. But again, from my understanding, many refer to dues as a portion they have set aside or plan to give God. And this does not qualify as a tithe.

I truly believe this misunderstanding has caused many to suffer needlessly in physical and financial areas of their lives. As much as it may hurt, God is not only a God of mercy, but He must abide by His Word. He is immutable regardless of the situation or the age of a person. Malachi 3:6 states, "I am the Lord, I change not." Therefore, His laws are immutable, and we will all pay a price if we do not heed them. This includes the young, the middle-aged, and the old.

So I appeal to the elderly in this closing section of this accountability chapter to get yourselves in order with paying your tithes and offerings, or you will continue to live way beneath your privileges. God's grace and mercy has kept you for many years. For this reason, you should be more than willing and obedient to show your love and reverence toward God's Word by giving tithes and offerings.

I know you are saying right now, "I live on a meager income, and I can't afford to eat or even stay cool in the summer and warm in the winter. I can hardly pay my insurance and keep food in my mouth, let alone my doctor visits." My parents had concerns exactly the same as yours. So my heart—and the hearts of many others—goes out to you. This world system has not been kind or fair to you. But God is more than fair! This is why you must become accountable and obey His Word. Just as it is for me, so it is also for you. Remember, God is no respecter of persons. And age will not exempt you from obeying what He has commanded **all** to do.

You see, if you don't accept Jesus as your personal Lord and Savior, regardless of your age, you will spend eternity in hell, and there is nothing God can do about it. But God has provided a way of escape! And just as He has made a way of escape for all to live eternally, He has also provided a plan to keep His people's financial provisions flowing. This applies to the elderly. Salvation renders blessings. So do tithes and offerings. God left us the plan of salvation and the law of sowing and reaping so we may receive His benefits.

The Widow of Zarephath: Our "Elder" Example

I'm sure God had real compassion for the widow of Zarephath and her son. Nevertheless, if she hadn't followed the law of giving to God *first,* she and her son would have died. God certainly wouldn't have wanted it that way, but His hands would have been tied if she had disobeyed the prophet's instruction. But she did obey, and her obedience opened the windows of heaven and poured out a miraculous blessing. And your obedience will do the same for you.

Many of you are doing a "good thing" in giving funds to your church in the form of dues. The good news is, if you give to God *first* what is His, He will deliver miracles for you that you can't even imagine.

Think About It—
WHEN THE WORLD SYSTEM FAILS YOU, GOD'S WORD WILL HAIL YOU!

The widow of Zarephath thought she was going to die. She and her son probably felt that no one cared. But God cared. He knew her situation. Yet, He couldn't *grow* for her until she *sowed* unto Him. She could have said to Elijah, "I'm just a lonely old widow with a son. It's just the two of us...why should we give you *first* that which is our last and only? How could you even ask for it? You ought to be ashamed of Yourself, God. With all that You own, You have the audacity to be greedy and ask for our last? Now I really want to die." And if she had said what the enemy wanted her to say—if she had pitied herself and her situation and chose to **hold** on to what little she had—both she and her son *would have* died.

But glory be to God that she gave! I am convinced that the account of this widow is recorded particularly for the elderly and others who may think they are exempt from obeying God's Malachi 3:10–11 law of the tithe for one reason or another. Circumstance has nothing to do with the immutability of God's commandments. This accountability teaching is intended to lovingly remind and wake up the elderly as well, so they can receive all they desire and need.

If you are such a one, you must give—to be given unto. You must release, even from your meager income, a tenth and an offering of it if you want to receive a miracle. You must trust and obey. God hasn't forgotten you; but you must release His hands to work for you. Remember, "…pressed down, shaken together and running over shall men give into your bosom" (Luke 6:38).

THINK ABOUT IT—
PITY AND SYMPATHY PAY NO DIVIDENDS!

Yes, God will move upon the hearts of men to render unto you what you need and desire. Pity is not what you need. Sympathy is not what you need. Neither of them pay any dividends. Miracles are what you need. And God is waiting on you with your personalized miracle.

So, let me remind you again: Paying *dues* is not the same as paying *tithes and offerings*. Satan has cunningly confused you, senior Christians. But God is exposing him to you now through this chapter. Satan has gotten away with this long enough. Our parents and grandparents didn't receive all that God had intended for them. Ignorance or the lack of knowledge robbed them of their seed and harvest. So enough is enough, Satan! We bind you up in the name of Jesus. Loose God's elderly in the name of Jesus!

Remember, man's system won't supply all your need and will certainly forget about any of your desires. The high doctor bills, medical bills, costly medicine, insurance, and housing are all man-made—and are the things that have been robbing you of your resources. So why continue to trust in them? You need a super-duper miracle, and only God gives those.

Are you ready to do what it takes, as the widow at Zarephath did, to activate God's blessings? Are you ready to believe and fellowship in God's financial plan? Haven't you had enough of man's failing ways? The more man charges, the less you get. You have nothing to lose, and I guarantee you by His Word that you won't be sorry. Just make sure you sow in good ground where the seeds are sure to sprout up—not in stony ground.

It is prosperity and wealth—not merely an occasional blessing here and there—that will fund our last-days harvest. And I don't know about you, but I want to walk in the wealth of prosperity, because God's blessings are manifested there.

God is a God of equality. Before redemption can take place, obedience must be displayed. When the children of Israel were leaving Egypt to begin their journey to the Promised Land, each person was given a half shekel to give God as an offering. Young and the old were allotted the same amount. And when the time came for them to release their money to God, it was required of the old to do the same as the young.

> The rich shall not give more and the poor shall not give less than half a shekel when they give an offering unto the Lord, to make an atonement for your souls.
> —Exodus 30:15

So you see, when it comes to receiving, everyone desires to receive an equal share or reward. But to do so requires your contributing equally as others do. Tithes and offerings are no different. This is why some prosper and others don't.

Remember the widow of Zarephath. Her obedience brought her out of dire need and into prosperity. God is not a respecter of persons. If you sow, He will make sure you reap. If you don't sow, however, you won't reap, and it will have nothing to do with God's being unfair. It will be because of what you did—or didn't do—to receive your just rewards according to His written Word.

I know I have pointed out some tough truths in this chapter on God's Financial Academy. Accountability is often a tough thing to confront. I also know that many of you may think I have been too tough. But truth is truth, and I do want to complete this chapter on a positive note, because God's Financial Academy is a positive course of study for those who will trust and obey.

> I praise you because I am fearfully and wonderfully made.
> —Psalm 139:14

The Word says that God made you fearfully and wonderfully. Do you realize the magnitude of this scripture toward you? God fashioned each of us as a unique work of art. A great minister, Reverend Spurgeon, once said, "The Lord fashioned you when no eye beheld you and the veil was not lifted till every member was complete."

Therefore, if we're that precious and valuable to God, certainly we should appreciate Him and value ourselves. Nothing should take precedent or stand comparable to us other than our Creator. No program, plan, or planning (except that of God's) should be satisfied until we've first satisfied His.

Yet, it appears that according to statistics, we shamefully

disregard our Creator—and His guidelines. This spills over into a poor self-image of *who* and *whose* we are. God faceted you to be the head and not the tail. You were bought with a most precious price. You were fashioned to be a royal priesthood, a chosen generation. You are children of a King—you're the King's kids!

If you are among the 20 percent of disobedient non-tithers, remain open and continue reading, and you will be blessed. If you are an obedient tither, there is much more to learn. You will learn things about our current government and financial institutions that will help you to think more properly. Not one of us ever completely "arrives" in the fullness of all that God wants us to know. We're all in His wonderful learning process. Let's move on to talk in the next chapter about the devourer. You may learn some things about Satan that you didn't know before.

Three
The Devourer of the Out-of-Order

Let's take a detailed look at the devourer who makes it his business to consume the finances of that 80 percent of church members and nonmembers will who let the other 20 percent do their giving.

> Look, a people rises like a lioness, and lifts itself up like a lion; it shall not lie down until it devours the prey, and drinks the blood of the slain.
> —Numbers 23:24, NKJV

God's Word tells us that Satan, as a roaring lion, walks around seeking whom he may devour. By taking a look at the definition of the word *devour,* we can see described what happens to a nontither's finances when the devourer comes in:

- "To eat like an animal"—*messy*
- "To consume, waste, or destroy"—*wasteful*
- "To swallow up, engulf"—*total consumption; never enough*
- "To absorb wholly"—*loses it all*

Building Wealth Using the Tin Can Method

Nontithers open the door wide through their disobedience, and the devourer walks through, wreaking havoc. His attacks are messy and wasteful, and he is never satisfied. One can go from big money...to little money...to no money—because the devourer leaves nothing untouched. He devours it all! The Amplified Version states it clearly: "Be well-balanced—temperate, sober minded; be vigilant and cautious at all times, for that enemy of yours, the devil, roams around like a lion roaring [in fierce hunger], seeking someone to seize upon and *devour*" (1 Pet. 5:8).

Take note that the Word says Satan is like a roaring lion, seeking *whom he may devour*. It says "whom he may" devour, because he doesn't have the right to just jump in and devour your finances. No! He needs permission and admission, which can only be gained through your disobedience.

Characteristics of the Devourer

As you learn more about the lion's characteristics, you will discover why God chose him as a representative of Satan's devouring ways.

The lion is a beautiful beast, mane and all. Isaiah describes Satan as the most beautiful of all angels and a gifted musician who could mesmerize with music. The Word says the fallen creature *appears* as an angel of light. And as it is with Satan, so it is with the lion; it is handsome, yet deadly.

But we all know that Satan is no "angel" by a long shot. So it is with a lion; it may appear handsome from its outward appearance, but when it opens its mouth, a real devourer is displayed. God says man looks on the outward appearance, but God looks on the inward heart (1 Sam. 16:7). The information in this chapter will help to steer you clear of the *false* appearances of Satan so as to not be so readily fooled.

The Master Predator

Remember, a devourer is a master predator, with fangs to devour both you and your finances. He has big teeth—"all the better to eat you (and everything you own)."

"Oh, what big teeth you have," you may say when a hungry devourer approaches. But once he sinks his teeth into your finances, only God has the power to deliver you from his deadening grip.

Piercing Eyes

It is said that during the day the pupils of a lion are scarcely more than slits. But as the daytime becomes night, the iris begins to open. By nightfall, its pupils fills its eyes. When darkness surrounds the jungle, not even the faintest glimmer escapes the lion's probing eyes. A metallic luster found at the back of the animal's eyes reflects almost invisible light. These shining headlights make it possible for him to see his victims and catch them unaware.

A lion's vision is six times better than ours. This is needed to take down prey and inch away without being discovered or seen. In like manner, the devourer Satan can spot a disobedient, out-of-order, unprotected nontither almost supernaturally from afar! Those eyes roam to and fro, seeking whom he may devour!

The nighttime is a lion's time. A lion must surprise its prey by stalking it, and his attacks can be implemented better at night. Although a thief usually prefers the night, his thieving activities are not limited to night only. Like Satan, it is during the night that the lion fiercely displays its majesty and personality. It is under the veil of darkness, when one least expects it, that it is easiest for him to render a surprise attack.

Nevertheless, the lion doesn't always get its prey. It seeks what it may devour, just as Satan. When Satan attempts to overpower one of God's obedient servants, his grip doesn't stay fastened. All he can do is attempt to continue his squeeze—and attempt he will.

PARALYZING ROAR

It is said that when a lion roars, he holds his head to the ground, and the earth literally shakes from his powerful rumble. The terrific volume of his roar vibrates throughout the forest, causing the entire wildlife world to rock with his thunder. It is said that this beast's terror is more often heard than seen in the African night.

But when the devourer attacks, his strength can knock the breath out of his victim even before he begins to devour it. So it is with one's finances when Satan is allowed passage by permission and admission because of disobedience toward God's financial laws. Some lions attack very large prey, so the size of one's bank account is no deterrent. In near total darkness, when one least expects it in their finances, out of nowhere the devourer swings into action. Like the trillions that lie within the stock market, no matter how large the prey, just the wind from this enemy's powerful blow can create havoc in one's finances.

POWERFUL AND SMART!

Have you watched lions in movies or television and been mesmerized by the strength and movement of their shoulders as they walk and prowl about? The humps in the shoulders go up and down in a most riveting and powerful motion. Just this movement alone can render its victim motionless.

A lion is built for power more so than for speed, although it is also fast. And a lion is smart; the lion (devourer) knows how to size up its opponent. So it is with Satan in one's finances. He observes closely the one who is out of order.

THE DEVOURER OF THE OUT-OF-ORDER

Then when his deadly grip is fastened upon him (the non-tither), there is not much—if anything—the victim can do. Just as most animals are no match for a lion, Christians and non-Christians are no match for the devourer when he is granted admission.

Therefore, it is a matter of life and death to avoid this predator's fastening grips. One must steer far from him at all cost, or it will prove to be detrimental to one's health and wealth.

THE ULTIMATE OPPORTUNIST

Lions are opportunists, which is to say they will wait for the right time to attack and wreak havoc when their victims least expect it. This is usually when things seem to be going well. Lions prefer eating without having to do much work. This is another picture of Satan, who just waits for his victims as they play into his hands and move in his territory.

Eighty percent of Christians daily make it easy for this opportunist to devour them. His feast is constantly laid out before him. He doesn't have to worry about going hungry since he has more than enough surrounding him for the day, month, and year. How can you go hungry when 80 percent of the church is on your menu daily?

Yet did you know that if a devourer doesn't get food in a proper period of time, since he requires so many pounds of food per meal, he will surely die? I wonder why we don't starve him. Each could do his or her part by being obedient. We possess the power to render the devourer helpless. But as I have so often stated, having the power to change a situation but not using that power is the same as not having it at all.

If you had the option of staying far away from a lion, would you take that option? Or would you choose to match strength and wits with it? Remember, it's important to know as much as one can about an enemy (devourer) so as to make correct decisions on how to confront him or to avoid him by staying out of his territory.

"Jungle" Finances

Let's take a look at the lion's camp. The devourer's camp is a jungle with no sense of order. Found mostly in the African Sahara regions, lions are the most feared of all beasts—especially by other beasts. A male lion can weigh more than 500 pounds and measure as much as nine feet six inches from nose to tail. Unlike you, other beasts have no one to defend them from this devourer. These fearsome animals have been labeled as the *kings of the jungle* because of their strength, power, brutality, and massive grace. However, this fact shouldn't cause fear. One can view a jungle as being representative of an entanglement or mess—and an entanglement can be avoided.

How many times have we heard people refer to their finances as being a mess? Perhaps the "mess" has occurred because disobedience has opened the door to the devourer. The devourer loves "jungle finances." He's right at home in the midst of them. Only obedience can lead one out of his lair to untangle his or her life.

The Lion's Fame and Game

There are numerous animals much larger in size than the lion. Yet no other carries its title—*king of the jungle.* Even those larger in size stand in awe of him, knowing his attack could prove fatal.

So why was the lion given such a name? Perhaps because he has several regal characteristics or because he makes more noise than any other animal. It may be the fact that he mercilessly hunts, kills, and devours his prey. I think God chose to compare Satan to a lion because the devourer also comes to kill, steal, and destroy without mercy.

The Devourer of the Out-of-Order

This beast eats the heart and lungs of his victim first. One may say that he goes "straight to the heart of the matter"—as does Satan with one's finances. Next, he eats the thighs and the brisket; he even has the sense to prepare for the proverbial rainy day, covering the remains with rubbish and coming back for several days for more meals from his savings. He has more wisdom than many humans! He knows, as we should, that after he takes care of today's hunger, he can go back to his covering (tin can) to know he will survive another day.

Some lions kill cape buffaloes, elephants, and even hippopotamuses. Some simply prefer certain tastes. I believe there is also a parallel here. In the spirit realm some devourers prefer baby Christians who are disobedient. Others prefer yo-yo Christians (those who pay tithes this week but not the next). Still others prefer long-time disobedient Christians, the rich and famous, and the wealthy wicked. There is even a stronger, more experienced, specialized devourer that is loosed to devour enormous wealth.

No One Is Immune

Remember, the devourer is watching, waiting, and stalking for just an opportune moment to attack, jumping on large mammal's backs and biting into their spine. *So listen!* You too—you "wicked rich"—are no match for the devourer. No matter how many millions and billions of dollars you have, your wealth can be devoured if you are not in order. Satan will jump you. And when he does, the only way to stop him is by getting in order through obeying the Word of God.

Depending upon the accumulated wealth of his victim, the devourer may take more time than is ordinary to overpower one's holdings. But Satan has many methods to get the job done—even some never before thought possible. Remember, he's a **master** predator, and he's good at his job!

Building Wealth Using the Tin Can Method

When the king of the jungle brings down an elephant, that elephant does take longer to die than a smaller animal. So it is with great wealth versus little wealth.

For example, when the "dry" season comes upon our government's world system (see chapters 7–9 for more detail), in order to keep their bureaucracy afloat, the "powers that be" will seek the money giants through creatively devised methods. This will begin a *survival of the fittest,* as world history as we know it draws to a close.

When one gets down to the bottom and has exhausted all other available assets, he begins to look toward that which seemed untouchable before. One begins to seek new territory. Out of desperation for survival, one begins to travel to the high lands, leaving the low lands. So it is with lions—and so it is with our governmental system.

There Is Deliverance!

A lion (devourer) can walk on his toes (which are like soft, fleshy cushions) so quietly that no one except God can hear him coming. He doesn't give his prey a chance to brace for danger. He senses his way by using his whiskers, which are equipped with sensitive nerves at each root. They measure the width of tight places and alert him when he has room to slip through.

Quietly and without warning, the devourer could create a personal or national financial crisis by catching millions off guard (as in the recent stock market plunge). A quietly developed tax law or some other unexpected attack could come out of Washington without warning, creating chaos in the nation. It could happen so fast that no one would have time to brace themselves. What would you do?

What are the things that could signal that a person has wandered into the lion's lair through being out of order? Bills thought paid years earlier—and even new unexpected ones—could surface. A need for major car repair—or even a new car—may arise. Major home appliances may break down, or some other unsuspecting need may present itself. When these kind of things happen, be aware, *the devourer is on the scene!* He has positioned himself, lying in wait for the disobedient until the opportune time when they become vulnerable, and then he strikes!

The Ultimate Slasher

Attached to the devourer's toes are weapons (claws) more powerful than a gun in the hands of a gangster. He has five on each forefoot and four on each rear paw, and he needs only to lift a paw to rip into his victim (your finances). When he pounces, four or five long razor-sharp claws strike and flay his victim (our finances) without mercy. When he goes into heavy action with all eighteen razors operating, (this fierceness is the type of attack I believe will be launched onto the wealth of the wicked) there is little chance for his prey. When the claws are not in use, they are neatly folded away until needed.

Think About It—
  No one ... I repeat ... no one is so secure in their finances that something or someone can't wipe them out. The devourer is prowling for those caught in jungle nets.

Computer Claws? The Y2K Crisis

Let's take our comparisons just a little further and think about the role computers play today in *controlling* and, yes, even *devouring* our finances. Most corporations and businesses are currently operated by computers—especially banks. Think about what would happen if an electrical

Building Wealth Using the Tin Can Method

power or blackout occurred. Do you think you could get to the bank and withdraw funds? Nine times out of ten, they probably wouldn't give you a dime. Why? Because they would have no way of verifying what's in your account and no way of identifying you. To the bank, you are an account and social security number. You gave up the right to your name when human tellers were replaced with robots and computerized machines.

Today, computers tell you what you can have, and what you can't...who you are, and who you aren't. Even if bank officials have personal knowledge of the fact that you have money in their vault, your transaction may not be honored because of the computer shutdown. A bank teller could only tell you, "I'm sorry, sir, but there's nothing we can do until the computers come up." Or worse, "I'm sorry, ma'am, but our account shows your balance at zero." It's difficult enough getting your money out of the bank under the best of conditions. A financial catastrophe would be horrendous.

Man today depends so much upon *mammon,* and he believes that everything he has made or done is foolproof. But 1 Corinthians 2:5 states that your faith should not stand in the wisdom of men, but in the power of God.

Don't you know that God, the all-powerful one, can cause a worldwide power shortage and shut this nation down overnight while you're sleeping, if He chooses? All the information in every computer could vanish. Whom will you call and depend upon then? What would you do if your credit cards or cash reserves showed zero because of a shutdown—but your baby needed milk and your family needed food?

In such a crisis, one had better know *Jehovah Jireh* (our Provider) and *El Shaddai* (our All-Sufficient One)—especially to the point of tapping into His wisdom, for wisdom is certainly what will be needed. *El Shaddai* has always provided a way of escape for His obedient people. He speaks powerfully and is a deadly shot. Only He can kill the lion

THE DEVOURER OF THE OUT-OF-ORDER

once we empower Him (with our tithing obedience) to intercede for us. When He rebukes the devourer, your electrical power will miraculously continue to work. He can insure that you have available cash on hand by inspiring you (for some unknown reason) to withdraw X amount of dollars from your account before a crisis occurs.

Don't think this is a far-fetched scenario. If the children of Israel's clothes and shoes didn't wear out during the forty years they were in the wilderness, this shouldn't be considered difficult for God to do. Remember the words of King David when he said, "I have been young, and now am old; yet have I not [*never*] seen the righteous forsaken nor his seed begging bread" (Ps 37:25).

Your wealth could be wiped out literally overnight by the devourer. This is why you need to be in order with whatever you have. Whether you are poor or rich—the first step of tithing supersedes all others. The other steps of order are only workable after the first has been taken.

God will allow those who are obedient to prosper in the midst of the storm. This world system based upon greed at the expense of the weak will collapse unless it's changed. God's Word tells us that a change is going to come. But don't fear! Simply *get in order and get ready*. God will handle the devourer for His obedient ones!

DANIEL AND THE DEVOURER

The story of Daniel is a good example of one who "devourer-proofed" his life. The devourer attacked Daniel, but he couldn't hold on to him because Daniel was in order.

> Then the presidents and princes sought to find occasion against Daniel concerning the kingdom; but they could find none occasion nor fault; for as much as he was faithful, neither was there any error or fault found in him.
> —DANIEL 6:4

Building Wealth Using the Tin Can Method

Daniel was well favored by King Darius, just as he was by previous kings, because of his wisdom, knowledge, and temperament. King Darius even had plans to promote Daniel over the other high officials of his kingdom. So Darius's cabinet hatched a plot. They established a royal statue that made it illegal for anyone to pray to any god except King Darius over a thirty-day period. The penalty for violators would be the lions' den.

Of course these evil men already knew of Daniel's constant devotion to almighty God. One of Satan's methods is to prey upon God's servants.

In Daniel's day, a lions' den was used as a powerful, inescapable, fatal tool of cruel punishment. Spectators often watched as the lions tore apart their victims and devoured them. No one ever escaped or survived the lion's den.

The royal officials did entrap Daniel, because he continued to pray to God three times a day. When the king realized he had been coerced into supporting such a law, he no doubt realized that it was a plot to entrap his friend Daniel. But according to the laws of the Medes and Persians, a signed decree from the king could not be altered. So the king began to set his mind on delivering Daniel:

> Then the king, when he heard these words, was sore displeased with himself, and set his heart on Daniel to deliver him: and he laboured till the going down of the sun to deliver him.
>
> —Daniel 6:14

Note the word *deliver* in this verse. Remember, who can *deliver* one from the mouth of the devourer other than God? He is the *Great Deliverer*. The king's attempts to save Daniel failed, and the penalty had to be carried out. Daniel's fate, it seemed, was sealed, and he was thrown into a den of lions.

THE DEVOURER OF THE OUT-OF-ORDER

Daniel 6:17 states that a stone was placed over the opening of the lions' den, and the king sealed it with his signet ring and the rings of his nobles. Daniel's fate could not be changed. The king somehow knew that the only one who could save Daniel from the devouring lions would be almighty God Himself, in whom Daniel believed. Isn't it funny how even unbelievers suddenly know that calling upon God is the only course of action when nothing short of a miracle is needed? Until such a hopeless situation, they claim there is no such God or miracles.

But as Malachi 3:11 says, "And I will rebuke the devourer for your sakes, and he shall not destroy the fruits of your ground" (even if he attacks you). Only God was able to save Daniel from the lions in that den.

At dawn the king, who fasted throughout the night, went to the lions' den, hoping against hope that he would find Daniel alive. The king cried out, "Daniel, you servant of the *living God!*" And Daniel answered, letting him know he was still among the living. The king, although an unbeliever, knew of Daniel's allegiance to his God, and therefore addressed him..."Daniel, you servant!"

Daniel had served God through obedience—which obedience warranted his deliverance from the devourer in his time of need. Daniel was in right standing. The New International Version of the same scripture indicates that the king asked, "Has your God, whom you serve continually, been able to rescue you from the lions?"

What if Daniel had not been a continual and obedient servant of God? I believe he would have become mince meat—a feast for the lions, for sure! But he was a continual, obedient servant and therefore was able to answer the king with confidence: "O King, live forever. *My God* has sent His angel and has *shut* [rebuked] the lions' mouths so that they have not hurt me." By his response, Daniel was implying, "*I was in order.* I have been obedient to God's law. Therefore, God shut the mouths of the lions (devourer) on my behalf."

Building Wealth Using the Tin Can Method

I believe the conversation in the lions' den may have gone something like this when God showed up: "Hello, My creation, you beautiful lions. Have you become acquainted with My servant Daniel? He seeks My face three times a day. I like that. He puts Me first before anything and anyone. I wish more of My servants would do this. Daniel is a fine example of how all men should be. Oh yes, you may wonder why I've shown up personally. Remember, I will always show up personally to rebuke on behalf of those who obey Me and are in order. Now I command you to be nice to Daniel while he is down here among you. Make your bodies comfortable for him to sleep on if he so chooses. He'll only be here overnight. I know you're hungry. You'll get the chance to eat soon, for those disobedient, out-of-order ones who plotted against My servant Daniel will become a feast for you instead of Daniel—and there are many more of them!"

And the lions' meal was served before lunch! Daniel's accusers and their entire families were thrown into the den. We're talking about wives and children here. So you see, it's not good to hang around sin in any form, for the sin of one will affect others. Remember, this was the case with Achan, Ananais and Sapphira, and with Adam and Eve. The sin of one will most assuredly affect others. The spouses and children of Darius's royal court probably had no idea of their culpability in this matter, yet they too were devoured. So again, it is important that the head of a household be in order!

Unfortunately, life is truly about the survival of the fittest. So when desperation comes knocking at your door in the form of a devourer, you will need God's supernatural power to halt its attack. For the obedient ones, God will step in and do the honors. As He did for Daniel, He will shut the devourer's mouth. Our almighty God is no respecter of persons. But, in order to rebuke the devourer for your sake, you must display obedience.

THE DEVOURER OF THE OUT-OF-ORDER

So don't forget: The devourer knows if and when you haven't paid your tithes and offerings. Such disobedience can signal when to strike. When a large bill comes, causing one to fear man more than God, and he pays the bill instead of God's tithe, the devourer senses the disobedience, and his whiskers become alert.

The peak of a lion's excitement is when it makes a kill. Satan the devourer smiles when he brings the finances of people—especially God's people—into his captivity. He enjoys killing and destroying one in any area of finances. If he has to use drugs, alcohol, or sexual promiscuity to do it, he will. Just like a lion, Satan isn't choosy about how he brings down his prey.

Pay your tithes. No devourer will be rebuked if this isn't done. Neither will the tin can method work to its fullest potential. Yes, the devourer is loose, alive, and well. And he is not afraid of your millions or billions. Your money doesn't scare him. It actually makes him salivate. "The more the better" is his attitude. He will get around to your account—you're on his menu! He prowls around *seeking* someone to devour (1 Pet. 5:8).

Judgment is coming! From the White House to your house—it will come to those who don't display order and devourer-proof themselves and their families.

Paying tithes and offerings is the blood application needed to detour the devourer from your door. God has given us the authority and the ability to come against and defeat many things here on earth by using the power invested in us through the shed blood of Jesus. Luke 10:19 says, "I have given *you* the power to trample serpents and scorpions." He also says that if we say or speak to the mountain to be removed and cast into the sea, it will obey us (Mark 11:23–24).

Remember the scripture in Malachi 3: "I [meaning God] will rebuke the devourer." Why did He say "I"? Because the devourer is such a nasty, evil force that only God can contend with him. But we can avoid or escape the devourer and put him out of commission by displaying obedience, which will inevitably cause him to starve.

I will repeat this over and over again so you may not miss it: Tithes and offerings are so powerful that they release the hand and power of the King of kings, enabling Him to rebuke the king of the financial jungle. Our obedience in this area isn't for God's benefit; it is for ours.

In this chapter I have unveiled the danger and predatory nature of this devouring beast. Let there be no mistake about it: He will, if we are out of order, wreak havoc on our finances without remorse or mercy once we stumble into his part of the woods. But praise be to God, he is no match for the King of kings!

If you are reading about the devourer for the first time, once you read these words taken from God's Word, you are now accountable for that which you have read. Obey the Word immediately to avoid any devastation, destruction, or ruin. *Get your house devourer-proof!*

In chapter 4 we will see what is involved in getting yourself and your house devourer-proof. Get prepared to build wealth, set up your own tin can, having first laid a solid foundation of obedience.

Four
The Power of Obedience

Have you passed a penny lately? Is it now clinking with the other change in your pocket? Or did you leave it on the ground where you saw it?

How many times have you passed by a penny on the streets, in the corner of your home on the floor, or in other unexpected places and just unmindfully stepped over or walked right past it, never giving it a thought? Maybe you thought:

- *A penny is insignificant and worthless; it's needless to stoop and pick it up. After all, what can it buy?*
- *Stoop and pick up a penny? I'm not so much in need that I have to stoop and pick up a penny.*
- *I'm looking for big bucks!* (So why are you giving them away one penny at a time?)

Perhaps you've even passed by a nickel on the ground and didn't stoop to pick it up. Even a dime or a quarter. But remember, in every dollar lies a penny.

Building Wealth Using the Tin Can Method

Think About It—
If you don't respect a penny—you won't respect a dime—and if you don't respect a dollar—poverty is just a matter of time.

Pay Yourself!

Now let's talk a little about you. How do you feel about you? Do you think you're worth the kind of finances God really wants to invest in you? Do you like and admire yourself? You don't think you're a mistake, do you? I should hope not! Because God made no mistakes when He fashioned you. In fact, His Word says that you are fearfully and wonderfully made (Ps. 39:14). He meticulously shaped your nose, lips, feet, and other body parts. He sat back and said, "Hmm, I think she'd look good with black hair." Or, "He'd look marvelous with blue eyes." Then He equipped each of us with our own unique personality. He gave us abilities, capabilities, and talents. When God made mankind He was actually "showing off." Therefore, because God fashioned and packaged us the way He did, we should feel good about ourselves.

And this should carry over into our finances. After we pay God His tenth, the next person in line to pay should be ourselves.

No One After God Should Be More Important Than You

After you work hard for eight or more hours a day and wait to get paid once a week, biweekly, or monthly, you should then pay *yourself* something. Don't put yourself on the back burner. If you do, it is indicative that you don't think much of yourself. You should be number one—after God—when it comes to your finances.

Other than God and our family, nothing is more personal than our own finances. So why, when we get that paycheck, do we cash or deposit it and then head straight to pay everyone else except God and ourselves? Who worked for the money? You did, of course.

Render unto God first that which is due—then render yourself a portion too. You're worth every penny of it! The tin can method will raise your consciousness and teach you to value every penny, because pennies add up to thousands of dollars when they are amassed. When God begins to bless you and your savings begin to grow, be ready to resist the devourer's temptations to hoard God's blessing. Always be ready to support others' needs.

> One man gives freely, yet gains even more; another withholds unduly, but comes to poverty.
> —Proverbs 11:24, NIV

Hoarding

Let's talk about hoarding. There are many reasons why we should save, but none of them involve hoarding. *Hoarding* simply means:

H olding
O nto
A ll
R esources
D oing
I nfinitely
N o
G ood

Because God loves you, He wants to prosper you. But your prosperity will only come as you repeatedly *sow to grow*. No *sow,* no *grow*. The opposite of sowing is hoarding. The law of reciprocity doesn't work in hoarding. Hoarding is sin and evil. We must release into the kingdom of God what belongs to God so the blessings of prosperity will continue to flow in our lives. Releasing the funds God blesses us with insures our continuous flow to grow. In other words, when you take care of God's business, He will take care of your business. This includes your children as well. David said in Psalm 37:25: "I've never seen the righteous forsaken, nor his seed begging for bread."

Admittedly, there is a very thin line between saving and hoarding. Webster's Dictionary defines *hoarding* as "to collect and lay up, to store secretly." So the mind-set of a hoarder is totally different from that of an obedient tither/giver who may also be a saver. A *hoarder* will probably never tithe because this would lessen his collection greatly. But nothing a hoarder may attempt to hide or store away is unknown to God. The Word clearly says that there's nothing hidden that shall not be uncovered (Luke 12:2).

A *tither,* on the other hand, is one who saves, yet knows the advantages of releasing funds whenever instructed by God so an even greater accumulation may take place.

A saver who is a tither understands biblical economics and knows the gospel must be financed.

A saver who is a tither is not under a curse and won't experience the curse that takes place due to disobedience.

A tither who is a saver doesn't hide his savings, for he knows he must be prepared at any time to release his savings according to instructions given to him by God. He will be in a financial position to do so without hardship because of his good stewardship with what he has been blessed.

So if you are in order with your finances, hovering over them to insure their safeguarding is unnecessary. God is Jehovah Jireh, our provider. And He gives us increase to scatter among the needy.

Joseph the Ordered Saver

A good biblical account of godly saving versus hoarding can be seen in the life of Joseph. Joseph was given favor by Pharaoh to oversee the land and store up grain, fulfilling a dream Joseph received from the Lord in which he was instructed to save during seven years of plenty because seven years of famine were soon to follow.

There was a reason for this storing or saving. It was to insure the health, wealth, and provision of the people through the hardship years. Joseph didn't hoard food in order to safeguard it from others and to keep it all for himself; he stored it for *preservation*. And, had he not been an obedient steward over what God had entrusted to his care, many would have suffered and died.

Hoarding will prevent your leaving an inheritance for your children and your children's children. The curse that falls over your hoarding may cause many horrible things to happen. You may die before your time and enjoy very little of your wealth—if any. Your heirs may fight a lifelong battle over it. The one who does receive it may squander it away in a riotous lifestyle that benefits no one. His children may never get the chance to see a penny of it. It is also possible that bad health may befall the one who receives the inheritance, and not even the money accumulated from hoarding can buy health or happiness. All of these and many more may befall your family from the curse and evil of hoarding.

Fear Produces Hoarding

Save, yes, but always be ready to release it (through sowing) to bring back more into your possession as God instructs. You and your family will have a continuous, bountiful treasure of inheritance.

Jesus taught about an actual hoarder, best known as the parable of the talents (Matt. 25). Three men were given talents (sums of money) to multiply. Two of the stewards were obedient and released their talents to produce more. But the third steward hoarded (buried to hide) his talent. He didn't sow, so he didn't grow. In the end, his one talent was taken away from him. Not only that, but he was labeled as wicked and was forbidden to enter into his master's rest—to be cast out into outer darkness—because what had been entrusted to his care was lost. So this hoarding business is serious business.

What the unfaithful steward hoarded could have produced an increase. It could have insured provision for him and his family, as well as promotion. So you see, what you think you may have from the accumulation of hoarding can be wiped out in a blink of an eye. Those who are stingy will lose every thing. Remember, *hoarding* is **H**olding **O**nto **A**ll **R**esources **D**oing **I**nfinitely **N**o **G**ood. And this is sin.

God has numerous, unlimited ways of blessing His people that our finite minds can't conceive. When you're a giver and are obedient to God, He will give you favor among men (Prov. 22:29). His hands are far from being short. What you can't do with $50, God can miraculously multiply to purchase one hundred times its normal capabilities. God knows how and where every good deal is, and He knows how to deliver it to your door, postage paid, if He so desires. How? Why? Because of his omniscience, omnipotence, and His goodness.

SIMON OBEY, AND LET DOWN YOUR NET

Simon Peter, a fisherman needed a miracle (Luke 5). He had been fishing all day and all night. That was his business, fishing. Nevertheless, on one of Simon's "business as usual" days, he couldn't get a catch. That's not good when you're a commercial fisherman! As a commercial fisherman, you depend upon your catch in order to make a sale.

Too many days without a catch will eventually shut down

The Power of Obedience

the business. On a day when Simon Peter was thinking he might have to close his business, God showed up and instructed him to try one more time. "Open up your business again," He said. But Simon felt hopeless. After all, knowing the business, he had tried everything he could. Simon was in the deep red.

Simon Peter was a master fisherman, and I can hear him saying to Jesus, "I know where and when to fish. I even know what time of day to fish as well. This is my profession. I'm a master at fishing. Other fishermen follow and learn from me. I've been out here all day, and I tell you—they're not biting!. Something is wrong. You stick with what You know, and I'll stick with *what I know.*"

But when God said to open up the "store" one more day, Simon Peter listened. Jesus told him to let down his net one more time—and his obedience produced a miracle. Simon obeyed and gave of himself. He denied his "better judgment," and swallowed his pride. Many times God comes at the very last moment so there will be no mistaking His blessing for anything other than a miracle. And Simon Peter was astonished, and discipled, because of what God did.

Today when retailers face the same challenges as Simon Peter—and respond in obedience—what happens? A miracle! What else? Our obedience, against the odds and our better judgment, invites God to show up at the nick of time, and we almost receive a sell-out. People begin to come from everywhere, out of nowhere.

God knows where all the **good deals** and **catches** are—and obedience can produce them. When God shows up to show us where these good deals are, we must prepared to act (and have a reserve of funds—even if it's just a little), because He is Lord and takes precedent over all. Even living creatures refuse to obey mankind out of reverence to Him. I believe the fish beneath Simon's boat sensed the presence of God. Even though they were always there (they had to be...where could they have hidden?) they refused to be caught until they heard Jesus say, "Simon Peter, let down your net." They knew by that statement that they were to be caught.

The Word says there were so many in that catch that Simon beckoned to his fishing partners to come and fill their boat. And as they filled them, both boats were on the verge of sinking because they weren't big enough for the catch (Luke 5:1–7). I believe it will be the same for you once you establish your tin can savings and exemplify obedience. Whether you understand or not—it's multiplication.

Can't you see the awesome glory of God? If the fish obey, the dead obey, and, according to Psalm 24:1 the rocks obey too, what is your excuse for not obeying? You are precious to God, and He wants to fill your boat (bank account). Obey what He has said, and let down your net today to receive your greatest catch. There's no way to *lose* by obeying Him. There's no way to *win* by disobeying Him.

MALACHI'S OBEDIENCE TEST

Actually, God has made a contest out of giving. When you challenge God in a test of giving He *always* wins. Simon Peter found this out when he obeyed Jesus' spoken word. Regardless of how much of an expert any of us become, we will never be able to defeat God in the game of giving. God is so amused by this in His Word that He challenges us to a test. He beckons us in His Word to play the giving game so He can continuously prove His unbroken track record. But we must play the game by following and obeying God's "giving game" rules.

So what must one bring to participate in this test? The rules and requirements can be found in Malachi 3:10. We must bring the first fruits of one's labor (tithes and offerings). This will qualify you to participate, and I guarantee that it will be one of your most enjoyable tests of all time. As you bring your tithes and offerings you pass! And the reward for your obedience will be God's giving back to you in such an immeasurable supply that you can't contain it.

The Book of Malachi was written to deliver stern rebukes to Israel's people—as well as their priests—to bring them to repentance and to stop their cheating. The defrauding of God in the tithes and offerings (cheating) has beckoned many curses in many forms to embrace our nation. To withhold honor and respect from God is to renounce His sovereign authority. It makes the disobedient as guilty as Lucifer was in the beginning when he failed his test. This imposes a curse so serious that a double curse was instated.

"You are *cursed* with a *curse:* for ye have robbed me, even this whole nation" (Mal. 3:9, italics added). When people rob God, in return they rob themselves. Their blessings escape, and lack comes on the scene. Malachi 3:10 must become permanently tattooed upon the hearts of those who want to please God. A bonding and everlasting kinship must be established toward this command if one is to remain and be rewarded in the testing.

> Bring ye all the tithes into the storehouse, that there may be meat in mine house, and prove me herewith, saith the Lord of hosts, if I will not open you the windows of heaven, and pour you out a blessing that there shall not be room enough to receive it.
>
> —Malachi 3:10

One must bring *all* the tithes. Those are the rules. But with many good-hearted Christians lies a major fault that causes disqualification. Many withhold that which rightly belongs to God because they think they might need it for economic hard times. This only causes more hard times, and it moves into other arenas such as sickness and disease. Satan will bring hardship.

Believe me, the devourer knows tithing works. If he

didn't, he would quit targeting this area. But tithing *does* affect Satan's kingdom, and that's why he works overtime to insure that we *disbelieve, discard, refute, neglect, and disobey.* You see, he loathes this money being used to support the work of the gospel—the gospel is his despised enemy because it exposes him.

God doesn't *need* your money; it's His money anyway, whether you work for it or not. He's not out to *break* you. He's out to *shape* you into His image. The giving of one's tithes and offering is an outward sign of one's obedience and subjection to God. That's why He restores back unto you an immeasurable supply, because God loves obedience and order and He loves to pass out A's on His tests.

Just as Malachi 3:10 should be reverenced and held dear to one's heart, so should Malachi 3:11. It will instill a healthy reverence and keep one on the alert to steer clear of the curse of the devourer. And it will keep one from receiving an F test score. Remember, God is the only one who has the power to contend with this prowler.

> And I will rebuke the devourer for your sakes, and he shall not destroy the fruits of your ground; neither shall your vines cast her fruit before the time in the field, saith the Lord of hosts.
>
> — MALACHI 3:11

The devourer (Satan) has such an insatiable appetite, that if allowed by you through your disobedience in withholding tithes and offerings, he will devour your very being. He will make sure you fail God's test.

God's tithing test is the hardest to pass some during times of adversity. Yet, it is when we learn to respond in times of crisis that God miraculously sustains us. Tithing is an act of faith, and it will flourish or diminish when natural circumstances tempt us to disobey.

The awful sin of withholding tithes from God today has

escalated into national proportions. So has the chaos.

The irresistible grace of God alone accounts for our continuous daily survival. So God is saying, "Test Me in the obedience test. Test My promises in this test and see if your obedience will not be rewarded!" The prosperity of our nation, if we would only obey, could be a witness to all nations of the blessings of obedience to God our Father.

I know many Christians and non-Christians alike who may argue this point by asking, "What's the use in honoring or serving God?" Just as in Malachi 3:13–15, many today also feel that evildoers seem to prosper more.

Some who defiantly and openly disobey Him appear to escape any punishment. And this *ghost appearance of truth* has caused many to lose heart. But I assure you, according to God's Word, that is just a fake appearance. For "God is not mocked, for whatsoever a man soweth, that shall he also reap" (Gal. 6:7). God is the expert of all expert recordkeepers. Don't ever forget that. He keeps a book of remembrance. **He is in the eternal record keeping and accounting business.** Malachi 3:16 indicates that no one—and I mean no one—who reverences, honors, worships, or obeys His commands will ever be overlooked. *God's memory is intact.*

So be assured that the righteous will be spared and distinguished from those who are evil when the day of judgment comes. Your obedience will never go unrewarded. And the disobedience of many will be dealt with just as surely. God will owe no man. In the day of "pay-up time" for the disobedient, the obedient will be spared because they are God's peculiar treasure. There will be a clear discernment between the righteous and the wicked. The righteous will never be forsaken. Of this we can be assured.

It is time to let down your net! The faithful will be blessed. There's no question about that. Those who persist in being disobedient will inevitably suffer and reap punishment upon themselves. But you don't have to be in that

Building Wealth Using the Tin Can Method

number! Will you pass the test? There is power in obedience, so adhere to this message, please! Those who have ears to hear, let them hear! The obedient will eat the good of the land.

The Power of Obedience

- *Obedience* can cancel all your debt.
- *Obedience* can cause you to own your bank.
- *Obedience* can cause you to become president of the company you work for.
- *Obedience* can cause you to own an airline.
- *Obedience* can cause you to reside in what you didn't buy.
- *Obedience* can cause you to own an island.
- *Obedience* can cause your child to be obedient.
- *Obedience* can cause you to discover on the moon what others could not.
- *Obedience* can cause you to find the hidden treasures of the sea, sought after by others, but not found.
- *Obedience* can cause you to discover the cure for the incurable, netting you billions.
- *Obedience* can cause your home to remain standing after an earthquake.
- *Obedience* can cause a hurricane to miss your property.
- *Obedience* can cause a stock market crash to devour every other stock, yet protect yours.
- *Obedience* can outwit your enemy.
- *Obedience* can cause your small steps of planning to become a spectacular success.
- *Obedience* can cause the ordinary to become the extraordinary.
- *Obedience* can cause you to become president of the United States.

THE POWER OF OBEDIENCE

Obedience is far better than sacrifice.
—1 SAMUEL 15:22

God remembers His own and knows how to distinguish them from the disobedient as any good teacher does. But will you pass the test?

Five

The Birth of the Tin Can

A fool with a little money will be the same fool with a lot of money.

It is time to birth your own tin can. It is time to start! I hope I have established the fact that God cares deeply about you and your personal finances, and that getting yourself in His order by following His financial guidelines is the key to personal success. Once you pass God's tithe test by bringing your tenth, His order of increasing the sum given in your obedience can begin. And once that begins, it is time to birth your tin can—and start accumulating the resources God entrusts to your care for His purposes. It's time to start paying yourself for the glory of God.

A tither who is a saver understands the fact that the gospel must be financed and understands the advantages of releasing funds whenever instructed by God.

Utilize any one of the saving plans in this chapter— START NOW...TODAY! For many of you it will be effortless. The only reason you haven't done it already is because of a satanic spirit called *hindrance* and an "Ah, it doesn't matter" spirit. They are both sent from hell. It's your future and your children's future; therefore saving does matter—so don't entertain these spirits.

The Birth of the Tin Can

Satan tells us the same "it-doesn't-matter" lie about salvation. He says, "Wait, not now, tomorrow." But the Word says *today,* not tomorrow, *is the day of salvation.* Satan wants you to delay anything that pertains to your good or benefit. He knows too well, better than we, that *delay will cause decay.*

So as you assess the following savings scales, showing what can be done when you make a commitment, don't delay; start today. Because of your obedience, God will surely repay.

To those who use well what they are given, even more will be given, and they will have an abundance.

$100 A Week Savings Plan

- $100 per week x 4 weeks or 1 month = a savings of $400
- $100 per week x 24 weeks or 6 months = a savings of $2,400
- $100 per week x 48 weeks or 1 year = a savings of $4,800
- $100 per week x144 weeks or 3 years = a savings of $14,400

How many of you today can say you have $14,400 in savings? I'm sure many have, just as I'm sure many do not. Of course, the tin can principle doesn't expect most savers to start at $100 a week. As I'll show later, you can start much lower. But some of you will find that often you squander more than $100 a week in many things today.

For example, dinner for two plus a tip could cost that on a weekend. Some have been doing this for years. Statistics show that few weekend diners have a savings. It's not that they don't make enough money to save. It's that many haven't established a financial savings plan.

I fell into this category many years ago. I was making enough to save $500 to $1,000 or more a week. Although I was making the money, it never occurred to me to establish a savings plan. I could not even tell you where my money was going. I couldn't account for its whereabouts. All I knew was that it didn't remain in my possession.

Now I understand that it was cursed because I wasn't in order. I wasn't giving my tithes and offerings. I was even attending church, but I didn't understand the reality of God's Word. Certainly I wasn't smart enough to pay myself regularly or consistently. And because of this, I had no desire to shape up. I didn't realize the severity of being under a spiritual financial curse.

But thank God for His grace and mercy! He knew that I didn't fully understand. At that time many people didn't even consider being blessed or prospered by God as a promise to be sought. Poverty and lack were considered holy.

God woke me up through a special encounter. He sent a young lady into my place of business approximately twenty years ago whose visit was so impacting that I need to take the time to share the story briefly. Out of this encounter I began to build my savings wealth using the tin can method.

I was the owner of a boutique shop that I established in the summer of 1975. I thought it was quite prestigious owning one of the few specialty ladies' shops in my area at that time. To me all that mattered was the fact that I owned and ran it. Whatever I made was just that—what "I" made. My understanding in the area of financial planning was zero, and it wasn't a concern. I had no saving mentality for the future, because after all, I had youth on my side.

I did have sense enough (thank God) to put aside enough funds to restock the shop for the next sales season. I had no bills at all at the time because I was single and living with my parents. At the time I didn't even own a car.

One day a young lady entered my shop and began to talk about an experience she had when her aunt asked to borrow some money. She agreed to lend it, but certainly expected to be repaid—since her savings were *only* about $16,000.

Sixteen thousand dollars! When I heard her say she had a

THE BIRTH OF THE TIN CAN

savings of $16,000, I began asking myself, *How could this young girl—who was younger than me, working in a factory "sweat shop," living on her own and supporting two children—have $16,000?* I was the cute "Miss Specialty Shop Owner" who was making more than she was—and I didn't have $16,000.

The idea seemed ridiculous! Yes, I shamefully admit that it blew me away. My heart and soul went straight to the very bottom of my stomach. I don't believe she knew how embarrassed and hurt I was. But I'll never forget that feeling. It shook me up. I made a decision then and there never to allow a factory worker—or anyone else—to outdo me as a business owner, especially when my income far exceeded theirs. I became obsessed about saving to avoid finding myself in that kind of predicament ever again.

There are several things I'd like to acknowledge here. First, I don't know how that young lady amassed the $16,000 she had at that time. For all I knew, it could very well have been from a small inheritance. I didn't ask, because if I had, I would have exposed myself in allowing her to know that she had more money than I did, and that would have been too painful and embarrassing. Nevertheless, I gave her the benefit of the doubt; I assumed that it was just plain common-sense saving and good stewardship. Looking back on it now in comparison to what God has taught me through the years, I know that consistent savings could have produced that kind of extra money.

I now understand that where you work or what you do has no bearing on saving or not. It's really up to you. Now, I also know better than to underestimate anyone's ability to save. This is why I challenge people to save. The people who appear to have nothing can be your greatest thrifty savers. We sometimes call them "penny pinchers." They may establish many little incremental savings goals in order to reach a certain level where they can modify their lifestyles until their savings goals are reached.

Building Wealth Using the Tin Can Method

I had not seen this lady for years at the time I started writing this book. But in my mind I said, *God, if this is of You, maybe I'll run into this young lady.* One day while walking into a Winn-Dixie grocery store I thought I saw her. I wasn't sure she recognized me, but as I passed by her she said, "Margarette, is that you?" (God is really something, isn't He?) He is certainly a discerner of your thoughts and the intents of your heart.

We came across each other's paths again on another occasion shortly thereafter. I didn't tell her about the book or the influence she had on me that day in the store. But now that this book is completed, I'm believing God will bring her across my path again so I can present her with an autographed copy!

The course of one's life can be altered by a simple meeting with a complete stranger. Mine was. And I learned to start where I could and with what I had. This is the wonderful simplicity of saving by using the tin can method. So must you, if you want to prosper. Don't be ashamed to start small, as Job said: "Though thy beginning was small, yet thy latter end should greatly increase" (Job 8:7).

Now here's your plan— just get a tin can, be diligent, and leave the rest to God. As I explained at the beginning of the chapter, maybe $100 a week is too large a sum for you to consider to start your tin can savings. But how about one dollar? How about two, four, five, six, or eight? Hopefully the following charts will inspire you to make your start:

 Your Tin Can Weekly and Monthly Savings Plans

- 1.00 per week x 4 weeks or 1 month = $4.00
- $4.00 per month x 6 months = $24.00

> Don't laugh at the $24.00 savings. It's a beginning and a very good one if you've never been able to save before. Remember, God will do the miraculous multiplying.

- $2.00 per week x 4 weeks or 1 month = $8.00
- $8.00 per month x 6 months = $48.00

This money can come from unnecessary expenditures such as sodas and gum. Don't "spend it" because you're accustomed to doing so. If you don't have a savings, you do now. To spend it would be self-defeating. I'll talk more about this in chapter 10. *Stay focused!*

- $3.00 per week x 4 weeks or 1 month = $12.00
- $12.00 per month x 6 months = $72.00

After paying your tithes and offerings, don't forget to continue to pray over your tin can savings for God to show you where and when to sow, enabling it to grow. Watch for **good deals** He will bring across your path.

- $4.00 per week x 4 weeks or 1 month = $16.00
- $16.00 per month x 6 months = $96.00

Keep going! You didn't get savings poor overnight, and you won't get savings rich overnight either. It's a process. Keep focused. God is with you this time.

- $5.00 per week x 4 weeks or 1 month = $20.00
- $20.00 per month x 6 months = $120.00

DON'T TOUCH IT! But you can smile.

- $6.00 per week x 4 weeks or 1 month = $24.00
- $24.00 per month x 6 months = $144.00

- $7.00 per week x 4 weeks or 1 month = $28.00
- $28.00 per month x 6 months = $168.00

Building Wealth Using the Tin Can Method

- $8.00 per week x 4 weeks or 1 month = $32.00
- $32.00 per month x 6 months = $192.00

- $9.00 per week x 4 weeks or 1 month = $36.00
- $36.00 per month x 6 months = $216.00

- $10.00 per month x 4 weeks or 1 month = $40.00
- $40.00 per month x 6 months = $240.00

Learn to start where you can with your tin can.

- $11.00 per week x 4 weeks or 1 month = $44.00
- $44.00 per month x 6 months = $264.00

- $12.00 per week x 4 weeks or 1 month = $48.00
- $48.00 per month x 6 months = $288.00

- $13.00 per week x 4 weeks or 1 month = $52.00
- $52.00 per month x 6 months = $312.00

- $14.00 per week x 4 weeks or 1 month = $56.00
- $56.00 per month x 6 months = $336.00

- $15.00 per week x 4 weeks or 1 month = $60.00
- $60.00 per month x 6 months = $360.00

- $16.00 per week x 4 weeks or 1 month = $64.00
- $64.00 per month x 6 months = $384.00

- $17.00 per week x 4 weeks or 1 month = $68.00
- $68.00 per month x 6 months = $408.00

- $18.00 per week x 4 weeks or 1 month = $72.00
- $72.00 per month x 6 months = $432.00

- $19.00 per week x 4 weeks or 1 month = $76.00

THE BIRTH OF THE TIN CAN

- $76.00 per month x 6 months = $456.00

- $20.00 per week x 4 weeks or 1 month = $80.00
- $80.00 per month x 6 months = $480.00

Learn to start where you can with your tin can.

- $21.00 per week x 4 weeks or 1 month = $84.00
- $84.00 per month x 6 months = $504.00

- $22.00 per week x 4 weeks or 1 month = $88.00
- $88.00 per month x 6 months = $528.00

- $23.00 per week x 4 weeks or 1 month = $92.00
- $92.00 per month x 6 months = $552.00

- $24.00 per week x 4 weeks or 1 month = $96.00
- $96.00 per month x 6 months = $576.00

- $25.00 per week x 4 weeks or 1 month = $100.00
- $100.00 per month x 6 months = $600.00

Your tin can now contains _____ ,yes, money!

You may say that this is elementary. You're right, it is. But many of you need to go back to grade school when it comes to your finances. These charts are simply supplied to give you an elementary look at the process. Whichever amount you can begin with on a weekly basis will be a wonderful start. Don't start too high and overwhelm yourself. If you can't begin with a dollar, then begin with twenty-five cents.

Think about the many churches that were built by our forefathers on nickels, dimes, fifty-cent pieces, and dollar bills. Years ago (and even some today), many church building funds began with small amounts of money collected

Building Wealth Using the Tin Can Method

consistently until there was enough for a down payment toward a new sanctuary. Churches focused on asking members to give a little consistently until it amassed into much, and God honored their obedience—the goal was fulfilled without rampant "can't-catch-up" indebtedness. Churches didn't get bank loans as frequently as today, throwing congregations into debt. Once a church signs on the dotted line, mortgage payments and rapidly accruing interest keep the hat passing day and night.

Today an *instant-gratification lifestyle* has overtaken America, including the church. And with that instant gratification comes *instant-debt bondage* that raises its ugly head.

Think About It—
Today our must-have-it-now mentality is steering many from the palaces to the pits.

In times past, people had more respect for what they had or had been entrusted with. Excessive indebtedness was considered taboo. Patience was regarded as a virtue worthy of respect. People envisioned, as we do today, the big picture, but they chose to take the *first step* toward it from the bottom of the stairs, instead of the top.

Patience cries out in distress to be heard. It's begging to prove its worthiness in our savings plans. Don't refuse to "let patience have her perfect work."

> The end of a matter is better than it's beginning, and patience is better than pride.
> —Ecclesiastes 7:8, NIV

Once you choose to grow persistently in the virtue of patience and remain in order, God will create the increase. Some may be able to do more, some less. For some an increase may not come every week. It may come every two or three weeks instead. Just don't become discouraged.

And, please don't think the tin can method is one of hardship or imprisonment. It's far from that. Some people will learn quickly how to balance their savings with God's increase and continue to indulge in the niceties they desire. However, for these people, it will be because of their salaries or their small amount of indebtedness. The only change for them that will need to occur will be to rearrange their order if they aren't paying tithes and offerings so as to avoid any future loss. Many may not be thinking of a savings plan and may not be prepared for tomorrow.

Remember, no one is so secure in their finances that something or someone can't wipe them out. This is why we need to be in order with whatever amount of money we have—from the poor to the rich.

The Power Behind the Little Stone

David is a good example of small beginnings. I'm sure you have either read or heard the story of David and Goliath. But do you realize that the little stone David used was not really what killed Goliath? It was the power that God invested in that little stone that actually killed the giant Philistine.

God's power is best displayed when small things are all we have—and miracles are needed. It didn't matter how much of an expert David was with that sling shot or how smooth his stones were. David simply didn't have enough strength in his mortal body to kill that giant. It was the awesome power of almighty God behind that little stone that sent Goliath sailing into hell. First Samuel 17:49 tells us that "the stone sunk into [Goliath's] forehead." What awesome power must have been behind that little stone! It had to be miraculous power, or it would have only annoyed Goliath and he would have continued his attack.

If you feel like your small beginning is as small as David's little stone against a Goliath, remember, it is not be the *amount* of your small-beginning savings that causes you to be blessed and prosperous. It is the awesome *promise* and *power* of God that causes it to multiply and do what it could never do alone. Just start running toward your Goliath as David did!

YOUR GOLIATH = A ZERO SAVINGS

Your giant is a zero balance savings account, but it too can be hacked. God will go before you to prepare the victory. And when people see you becoming victorious after they've said you couldn't do it, their attitudes will change. But they will change only after you do something to prove them wrong.

After we have won the victory in any battle, whether it's physical, financial, or spiritual, people will do one of two things. They will either run to you or run from you. In the case of finances, they probably will run to you for a loan of some sort. At the very least they will become inquisitive about how you did it. If they're unsaved, you will be able to use God's victory as a tool to witness and bring them to Christ. After they accept Jesus Christ as their Lord and Savior, begin to share the tin can method with them. Then as they prosper, they will take the same message back to their friends.

David became the friend of Jonathan, King Saul's son (1 Sam. 18:15). When you are obedient to God in small things, He will give you honor, respect, and favor among men. He will change your *associations*. The Bible also says that David prospered and behaved himself wisely, and that King Saul set him over the men of war. Not only did his associations change, but he also received *favor* and *promotion*. God's Word says the willing and obedient will eat the good of the land (Isa. 1:19). God will see to it that you're the head and not the tail (Deut. 28:13). He will cause people who perceive you as a *nobody* today to look at you in awe tomorrow when He makes you a *somebody* for His glory and honor. He will enable you to become a ruler over much if you will not despise your small beginnings. But it's a process. He has to see your obedience and faithfulness first.

> But God hath chosen the foolish things of the world to confound the wise; and God hath chosen the weak things of the world to confound the things which are mighty; and base things of the world, and things which are despised, hath God chosen, yea, and things which are not, to bring to nought things that are: That no flesh should glory in his presence.
> —1 Corinthians 1:27–29

Not only did David have only a small stone when he fought Goliath, he was also considered the least of his brothers. But he was obedient in the very first thing to which God called him—a sheep keeper—and he did that calling well. David didn't murmur and complain while tending the sheep. He didn't consider his job a menial task, nor did he disrespect it. David respected his position and did his job well. He didn't despise his day of small beginnings.

David was protecting his flock when he killed a bear and a lion. Many in that situation might have said, "Let the bear and lion eat it; I'm not going to risk my life for one small sheep against a bear and lion." But David was faithful in his job; he took it seriously. Just as you should take your tin can savings and small beginnings seriously. Once David proved himself, God promoted and anointed him to become the next king. Why? Because if he proved to be a good shepherd over sheep, God knew he would be a good king over His people.

David proved himself worthy of promotion, and he

received prosperity because he never complained about where he was, what he did or didn't have, or what he was doing. He proved himself a great warrior in defending a **small** thing, and God elevated and prepared him for **greater** battles.

Let us take heed! When those who criticized you about your small beginnings see how God has favored and prospered you for being obedient and acting wisely, they will react as Saul did to David. The Word says that when Saul saw how capable and successful David was, he stood in awe of him. The same thing will happen to you.

First Things First

The first steps of order—tithes and offerings—must be put first. No devourer will be rebuked if this command isn't honored. Neither will the tin can savings method truly work, because God is definitely a God of order. His words are His commandments, and they will not be changed. What God said, He means eternally. And the devourer is alive and well on planet earth.

Like David, You Will Also Have Your Critics

After a victory, your enemies will be plotting, criticizing, and setting snares just as Saul did with David because of jealousy. Look neither to the left nor to the right. Just keep your eyes on your Jehovah Jireh, and He will fight all of your battles, including your *giant* financial ones!

God's power is best displayed when small things are the only "availables" and miracles are needed.

God will prosper you as you pray about your tin can savings. If you commit to Him in obedience, He will honor His Word. So pray over your tin can daily. Pray:

Lord, according to Your Word, You will bless the

fruit of my labor. You will send blessings, and You will cause me to be at the right place at the right time. Good deals will come across my path, and I will know that it is by Your sovereign hand. I thank You for this, in Jesus' name. Amen.

Your friends and family may laugh and criticize when they see you praying over a can, but ask them if they have a better way. David was criticized for speaking out against Goliath, but no one else had a better solution—or was even noble or brave enough to try. The Philistine cursed David, but God stepped in to contend with Goliath. He will do the same for you as you pay your tithes and offerings, following the steps of God's order.

Goliath made a big mistake in judging David by his size. So it will be with your tin can savings. Many, including yourself, will misjudge it according to its beginning size. But when the giant came forward, David took his head off with his own sword and brought it back to the camp for all to see. I see you with your tin can holding it up for all the world to see saying, "It works! It works! I did my part, and God did His. He gave the increase and won the battle for me!"

Yes, God chooses the small things to defeat the mighty. Just like Saul, man thinks one must use big things to fight big things. Remember, Saul offered David his armor. But David told him, "I can't use these things because I haven't proven them" (1 Sam. 17:38–39). David hadn't tested the heavy armor, which was too big for him anyway. So he took it off and armed himself with what he knew had always worked for him. I can imagine David thinking, *I didn't have this armor on when I killed the bear and the lion. God delivered me from them. Therefore, I don't need them to fight this uncircumcised Philistine. I'm going to stick with what has always worked for me. Even though it's small, what counts is that it works.* Always stick with what works.

Building Wealth Using the Tin Can Method

So it was for me. My wealth today is a direct derivative of my simply applying that which I knew. I applied that knowledge well, did not despise my humble beginning, maintained consistency—and my savings giant was hacked! Now God in me is the Giant of my finances.

Just remember to be obedient with what you have. As you are, God will deliver the victory and bring on the unexpected miracles. The miracle of killing Goliath was surely unexpected by all who looked on. David used what he had, rejected the words of his naysayers, put God first, and *won the battle.* You can be victorious, too!

Think About It—
A SMALL SAVINGS BEATS HAVING NO SAVINGS AT ALL. NEVER FORGET: IT'S BETTER TO START SMALL THAN NOT AT ALL!

Six
Go to the Ant

Go to the ant, thou sluggard; consider her ways, and be wise.

—Proverbs 6:6

Why does God tells us in His Word to consider the ways of the ant? Why would man, who is much larger in size and supposedly a much wiser creature, have to consider the actions of a tiny insect like an ant? How can something so little possess so much wisdom? Its brain, if it has one, can only be the size of a pin point. Nevertheless, since the ant was created by God, He knows that this little insect has much significance that could be beneficial to man in some respect. Such significance warrants our study of the ant. He explicitly told us to consider its ways if we want to be wise.

Most of the time when you see an ant, you are likely to step on it or call the exterminator if you have an abundance of them. Once again we see the lack of respect that most people have for anything small—especially for small beginnings.

Ants possess attributes that people need in order to succeed—consistency, tenacity, and diligence. An ant doesn't say, "I can't do this or that because of my small size." Neither should you. Not only that, but an ant, though small, has a big or powerful bite. You know this to be true if

Building Wealth Using the Tin Can Method

you've ever been bitten by one. It hurts! Never forget that you can't judge the power something has by its size. The same is true of pennies, nickels, dimes, and dollar bills.

The ant is no complainer. The ant doesn't say, "Everything and everyone here on the earth is so much larger than me, so if I don't succeed it's because I was short-changed due to my size." Many people use their human reasoning to limit their ability to save because of the smallness of their income, saying, **"I can't save because of the size of my paycheck."** The ant doesn't worry about competing with other giant creatures. Don't give yourself room to complain by saying you can't compete financially because you don't have a large sum of money to start with in order to save.

When you study the ant, you will find it can only take **one piece** of something at a time back to its camp. Yet it never gives up. It keeps its focus and keeps going in stride with great diligence while storing up its food until it amasses a great amount. Although it may begin with something small, it continues to build upon that small beginning—until it eventually amasses something enormous. Even when ants reach their goal, they keep going—very much like the Energizer bunny that you see on television.

So the Lord has given us a lesson through the study of His ant from which we can obtain wisdom for human living. I don't know about you, but anything I can study that will enhance my wisdom—I want it. More importantly, I need it! Don't you?

> Go to the ant, you sluggard, consider her ways; be wise…which having no chief overseer or ruler, provides her food in the summer and gathers her supplies in the harvest.
>
> —Proverbs 6:6–7, AMP

The ant has no ruler, no boss to command it while

GO TO THE ANT

looking over its shoulder and pushing it to do more. So what motivates it? I believe it's the desire to succeed, the desire to stay alive and not get hungry, and the desire to depend on no one but itself—and it succeeds.

The ant knows what has to be done and does it. If it doesn't, it knows it will pay a price later. It knows it will starve in the winter if it doesn't gather during harvest time. Do we not need to recognize the truth in this?

I'm certain almost everyone has seen the little hills of dirt left by ants in sidewalk cracks or open fields. These ant hills, as we call them, surround the entrances to their underground nests. The hills vary in size according to the species that build them. Harvest ants are known to build hills two feet tall. Certain African ant species are known to build nests that reach enormous size over the years. One hill has been reported as being twenty-five feet tall! Here is another ant lesson concerning savings. With diligence, savings will evolve into an enormous size over the years. The ant doesn't give up—it is familiar with the virtue patience.

In the ground beneath an ant hill you will find many new rooms and tunnel systems. In a typical nest, each room has its own special use. The first room in the nest is reserved solely for the queen. It is in here that the queen ant continuously lays an increasing supply of eggs. This compares to the first place we must give to the first 10 percent of our income—which is reserved for the Lord's tithe. God will multiply them continually to bless us. This is His main focus for mankind. He will open up the windows of heaven and pour out blessings that we won't have enough room (storehouse room) to receive (Mal. 3:10).

Other rooms in the anthill serve as nurseries for the ant's eggs, larvae, and pupae. Worker ants carry the newly laid eggs in piles to these other rooms. There are many of these nursery rooms throughout the nest, and the nurses are always moving their young around (like stock market investors) to find the warmest, driest, best spot every day.

Building Wealth Using the Tin Can Method

Can you envision God's people having to move "piles" of money around daily, trying to find the choicest places to invest? God will replenish as soon as one empties out. Jesus said in Luke 6:38:

> Give, and it shall be given unto you; good measure, pressed down, and shaken together, and running over, shall men give into your bosom. For with the same measure that ye mete withal it shall be measured to you again.

In addition to having several nursery rooms, there are many storerooms in a hill. We must have such rooms as Christians if we're ever going to be the head, not the tail, lending to many but never borrowing (Deut. 28:12). When this happens God gets all the glory and honor!

So you see, the ant is driven. Diligence! It possesses diligence! The ant knows it has to store its food in the summer to provide for itself in the winter. What are you storing for yourself to provide for unexpected circumstances? What will you do when God says, "I want you to bless your neighbor"? What will you do when God says, "I'm sending you a good deal and all you need is $200 to obtain it"? Hopefully you will say, "Come here, my tin can savings, I have you for such a time as this."

A young lady recently called to say she desperately needed to see me right away. She gave no indication over the phone as to what the urgency was. When we met, she was exasperated and panting, with tears running down her cheeks. She blurted out her urgent need to get a grip on her finances. The woman told me that her husband worked two jobs and that her job paid a decent salary; she couldn't understand why she was suffering from a lack of money.

Many people constantly say that if their jobs paid them more, they could save. But this isn't necessarily true. It is true that we would all like to earn more. But for many, earning more doesn't always contribute to their saving more. For many, they are simply financially lazy.

I discovered that this young lady, who was a Christian, had no order in her finances. She didn't have many bills. But most importantly, I discovered that she had stopped paying her tithes and offerings, which caused her finances to immediately fall under the Malachi 3:10 curse. She had never heard of paying herself next after the tithe, and she certainly wasn't managing the payment of her bills. She had two or three small insignificant bills that could have been paid off immediately instead of paying the "required" minimum that only goes to interest. But again, she never once said she needed to make more money. In fact, as stated before, she admitted to having a well-paying job. In short, both she and her husband were suffering from being out of God's order. So my advise to her was to get back into God's biblical order.

Many of you fall under this category. You have been blessed with well-paying jobs, yet still you suffer lack in your finances. More money won't always take you out of your negative financial zone. Only God's financial plan will. You must pay Him first, and you must pay yourself something next.

The Change Is Your Choice

I have heard too many people from all walks of life chatter about how difficult it is to save. Many shout it from the house top, making statements like:

- "I just can't seem to get my hands on enough money to save. It's hard for a person to save these days."
- "If I could just get a decent-enough raise, I could begin saving."
- "I don't make enough on my job to save anything. I'll never be able to save anything anyway, so what's the use?"

Building Wealth Using the Tin Can Method

I must admit that I used to make statements like this before I discovered the tin can. The question is, Are these statements of truth—or mere fallacies? Do we use these statements as excuses to support our negligence, wastefulness, and poor measure of stewardship over our money? I think you know my answer to these questions.

A typical paycheck-squandering person who has a portion of his paycheck going directly into some type of a savings or retirement account would probably be lost if he had to do the exact same thing on his own. Why? If this "potential" savings money came directly into his hands, he would probably get lost in the shuffle of how to manage or spend it intelligently.

Undisciplined spenders will always put their own fingers into their own pot. Again we find the solution from the ant. The ant works hard to accumulate—not spend—and they do it for the good of others.

It's important to know how to manage and oversee your own money. Elementary things should be simple things. And if they are simple, they should be easy to learn and implement. Yet for millions of people, they're not. I've seen many people who can manage many things except their own personal finances. So take concern over your finances—I did. **More money isn't the answer. Managing it is.**

Take, for example, the following woman's testimony:

> I have always had well-paying jobs since college, and I have always been single with no children. As a child, my mother always encouraged (although she didn't teach...there's a difference) my sister and me to save, save, save, and we did. As an adult however, my mentality changed from save, save, save to spend, spend, spend. On an average, after taxes, I would bring home around $500 a week, sometimes more. This was after I had paid my car note, which was my biggest expense, and rent. If I got paid on Friday, by Monday I would

be practically broke. There was something about a Saturday that compelled me to go out and spend. Most of the time I didn't even need anything, but because I had some money, I felt as if I had to find something to buy. My mentality was that someone might be having a sale on something that I will need, so I'd better go ahead and buy it now.

I don't have a savings account. [She gave her testimony some time ago, so hopefully her status has changed today.] The real reason that I don't have one is because I never learned how to budget. I was always told that I should save, but I was never shown how to save. The sad part about it is that if I wanted to buy a new car today or if I needed to buy an airline ticket for an emergency or even if I needed to have some cash immediately, I would be in bad shape. Other than my paycheck, I have no available cash. If I had 5 percent of the money that I have blown away in the past six months, I could buy a car. If I had 1 percent of the money that I had wasted since 1988, I could buy a car, a house, and completely furnish the house.

There are thousands of people just like this young lady who need to go to the ant. Again, her job source was more than adequate to meet her needs. But she wasn't a tither and was undisciplined, so her disobedience embraced a spirit of loss upon her finances. Just as thousands of you, she had more than enough to give God and to save.

SAVING FOR OTHERS

Now let's look at something else that's quite significant in relation to saving that the ant has to show us. Ants have two stomachs (the *crop* stomach and the regular stomach) located in the abdomen's back section, called a *gaster*. The larger stomach, the *crop,* is also called a *community or social stomach*. Food is stored in this part of the stomach to share with other ants in the community. Can you imagine this? A creature as small as an ant, which is considered insignificant in size and stature, has the ability to store food for those who may be in need of substance. How many of us—God's prized handiwork, made in His image—have stored away not only a sufficient supply for ourselves and our families, but for others in our community as well?

Even more meaningful, the other ants in need don't have to buy anything or do some little dance step to earn their fellow worker's gifts, because they are accountable to one another. They are of the same kind, and say, "Hey, I have enough food in my house for your house. There is enough for me and anyone who is in need." This is a powerful truth. Ants truly are their brother's keepers.

Isn't it just like God to use the smallest of the creatures as an example for us? Could that be why we should not despise small things? Because small things can do gigantic jobs? The same applies to one's finances. Remember, "It's the simple, seemingly foolish things, that confound the wise" (1 Cor. 1:27). Don't despise small beginnings. Don't despise people you consider to be insignificant nobodies who have nothing to offer. And don't do it with your small change. Its bite and might just may be bigger than you give it credit for.

Most people are doing great just to have enough for themselves. So how can they be a blessing to someone else? It's good to be blessed. But it's far better to be blessed enough to give and be a blessing. The most important job an ant has is that of enlarging its nest to serve others, and this is what the tin can method is ultimately all about.

Why would one need to enlarge something? The need for more room is one reason, increasing our capacity so we can spill out on the lives of others. If you had a four room house and needed room for more, you would need to add another room to accommodate growth. Ants will begin a nest anywhere. They're not choosy. They will build them in telephone poles, rotten wood, logs, or just in the earth. They start with whatever they have around them, wherever they are. You and I can learn from the ant. When we are willing to start saving with what is available, enlargement will come.

Let's correlate this with our lives. What does God say in Isaiah 54:2–3?

> Enlarge the place of your tent and let the curtains of your habitations be stretched out; spare not, lengthen your cords and strengthen your stakes, for you shall spread abroad to the right hand and to the left hand, and your offspring will possess the nations, and make the desolate cities to be inhabited.
>
> —AMP

What is He talking about? He is saying, "Get ready for expansion and multiplication."

In applying this to tin can finances this means start where you are—put aside your small beginnings in a tin can savings, and God will do the honors of blessing and enlarging it through multiplication. He will open doors wide with what you have in a supernatural way. But you must show stewardship (tithing) over what you have *now*. You must be faithful and consistent in storing a portion of the little you have in a tin can savings after you have given your tithes and offerings. God will work out the rest. When our pennies, nickels, dimes, and dollar bills accumulate with God's blessing, we will be able to reach out and help someone else.

Don't forget: *Proper channels create accurate and definite results*. So don't try a shortcut—it won't work. Obedience is better than sacrifice. If the ant works diligently enough to create expansion by enlarging its nest, how much more should God's people be willing to enlarge, grow, and expand? God told Adam and Eve to be fruitful and multiply

(Gen. 1:22). He told Abraham that He would multiply his seed as the sands of the earth (Gen. 22:17). All God wanted was their obedience. At the time, Abraham probably couldn't envision the type of multiplication God was talking about.

Nevertheless, multiplication brings growth and progress. It also sets you in a position to be prosperous enough to bless others. When your tin can savings begin to spill over and you have to replace it with barrels, then there will be more than enough for your family. You will want to start another phase of investing. You will want to call your relatives, neighbors, and friends to share the good news with them. When it (the good news) starts to catch on, even the unsaved will be curious. You will be able to win them to Christ by the lifestyle you have been exemplifying. Then a chain reaction of blessings will start flowing into your life that will touch the lives of others.

Community Accountability

Did you know that despite man's feelings of strength and independence, he can't survive alone any more than an ant can? Aloneness can destroy you. Many people have died because of it. That's why God says it is not good for man to be alone. As strong as an individual ant is (it can lift 50 times its weight), it still can't survive as an individual. Its entire existence depends on the way it lives with a group. This is why ants are called "social" insects. In order to survive, they must work and depend on other ants in their community. They must assist each other in finding food, taking care of their young, and defending their camp from enemies.

So the ant provides another example of how God desires mankind to reside upon this earth—as personal and extended families all the way up to the national level. Mankind can't survive without God. We all need Him and should be dependent upon Him.

It takes numerous ants, each working together doing its

own special job, to keep their community alive, just as it is the responsibility of each individual citizen to assist in keeping this nation a living entity. We are our brother's keepers. That's why God wants us to be equipped financially to assist one another. When my sister doesn't have, I can go to my brother, my mother, my father, my neighbor, and my friend. He wants us to be stocked up in our storehouses so we can help ministries bring in the harvest in preparation for the End Times. Surely we don't expect Satan and his cohorts to help. We shouldn't be disobedient participants in his plans, nor should we be a part of his community.

God loved us so much that He didn't come to us in some complicated way or manner. He made all things, the great as well as the small. He made the whale and the ant. But He said to "go to the ant" for wisdom in living. He didn't send us His Son in the form of some riddle. Jesus came as a small child whom we could all recognize, understand, and identify with. He wanted to make sure that we perceived and received Him.

Don't forget: The ant begins with a *single small room* before it diligently expands. Here is a summary of the positive characteristics that make the ant successful:

- They are extremely organized.
- They have highly developed social abilities (interact well with fellow ants within their family or community).
- They are communicators.
- They are excellent workers (not afraid of hard work).
- The are great fighters and defenders.
- They possess harvesting skills (know how to store and gather).
- They are very adaptable (will and can live almost anywhere, except in extreme cold areas).
- They are sharers (share among their colony and are their brothers' keepers).
- They are great builders.

Building Wealth Using the Tin Can Method

- They are great reproducers.

Keep all of this in mind when the enemy tells you it's no use to start your tin can savings with a single small coin. **Your tin can may start with a single coin, but you have a heavenly Father who has given you guaranteed promises to multiply your seed beyond imagination.** He will give you the increase. It is up to Him to part the Red Seas, to open up the windows of heaven, and to pour out His blessings through the miraculous. All He wants from you is something He can work with. And your tin can is where it can all start.

You Do Possess Discipline

Because God created the ant as a responsible contributor to the good of its community, it is always available and ready to serve in its created capacity. It is disciplined beyond what most humans are able to hear or to bear. So here is yet another lesson God has for man through the ant. I hear too many Christians and non-Christians alike complain about how they find it difficult to discipline themselves to work toward building a savings. Yet these same people seem to be able to pull very good discipline habits out of a hat in order to indulge in many nonproductive, unfruitful things. This nullifies the "I-can't-save" cliché. People of every race, color, creed, and financial status do *what they want, how they want, if they want, and when they want!* But excuses and abuses abound. Someone else is always at fault when they can't do this or that. Their mental wants overshadow any ability to use common sense. They rank many things as top priority over God and their own personal welfare. Many give lip service to God, saying He is number one—but their actions beg to differ. In any scientific study, you will never find an ant looking out for number one.

We all have discipline that we often choose to exercise in one way or the other. Saving can insure and secure the livelihood of one's future and the future of that person's children, so saving must become a discipline. As we look at some financial disciplines that most people choose every day, I think you'll find that they definitely nullify the "I-can't" cliché. With the discipline and consistency of an ant, we diligently work to insure the following regular payments to meet our obligations and keep our credit records clean.

LIFE INSURANCE VS. SAVINGS

Let's look at life insurance first. Many people who claim an inability to save consistently have paid insurance premiums consistently for years—be they large or small—without fail. Yet they say they can't consistently pay God in the giving of their tithes and offerings.

What's the difference? A cost is a cost and an obligation is an obligation. What's really at issue is what or whom you value the most. This is known as *prioritization,* which means "what or whom you respect or reverence more; to what or whom you're more faithful."

Disobedience is just that—disobedience. Disobedience produces disorder, which will eventually demand that a price be paid. We harbor many excuses within ourselves, but excuses will work against you.

Insurance companies work very much like a savings account, but they are set up to be more advantageous for the insurance company than for you. We have been programmed to put much faith and trust in this institution. Some types insure that you are provided for in a time of crisis. But many do not. I believe many people, Christians and non-Christians alike, are insurance crazed. And most policies don't do you any good *until you're sick or dead.*

What about when you are *well and alive?* Why can't you enjoy life while you are living? Why bank on someone else enjoying life after you're gone at your own expense? Why can't we enjoy life together?

Building Wealth Using the Tin Can Method

Some of our elderly are depending upon a type of life insurance policy for which they have more than paid the policy's yield according to term. This was true of an insurance policy my parents had years ago. It was a $1,000 policy, which, at the time they purchased it, sounded like a nice sum of money if something should happen. Back then things were very inexpensive, so $1,000 was considered a nice sum. I recall an insurance lady coming around monthly to collect the two-dollar premiums. Because of the faithfulness of their agreement, they paid much more than what the policy was worth. You see, two dollars a month for ten years would have been $240. Therefore, $740 is what was left on the policy's value. So they basically could have saved their own $1,000.

Yesterday, as it is today, there were many insurance agents who didn't care about educating the elderly. Much more emphasis was often placed on selling and overselling insurance policies than on financial guidance and sensible, truthful education. The same thing is true today. Many have been conditioned to pay senseless premiums faithfully for years. And to do this, they show discipline.

Most people have the mentality that in case they die, their life insurance moneys will be available for their remaining families. The fear of this naturally drives them to maintain consistent payments. In many cases this is probably good, especially if the person had to put aside the same premium in a savings account.

We're masters at paying others faithfully instead of paying ourselves. Most insurance companies are merely savings accounts. But all the money you pay them on a monthly basis accumulates a handsome interest for the insurance company—so that they make even more money by investing your money, too.

Now, of course, it's true that if you should pass on, the premium will be paid to your family. But you had better believe they have calculated as precisely as possible the time of your passing to make sure they have invested and made the most money possible while you are still alive. They don't make money from your death. Remember the physical you took?

I'm not talking negatively about insurance companies. The point I'm trying to make is that we should strive to save for ourselves and make our own investments to reap the benefits. Why do we place more confidence in making payments to man's creative financial institutions than we do toward the things of God? If you can pay an insurance premium of $20 a month for fifteen years, how difficult can it be to pay yourself (tin can) $20 a month for fifteen years? That's less than a dollar a day.

The following chart represents other payment disciplines people faithfully maintained for years.

TYPE OF PAYMENT	NUMBER OF YEARS	COMMENTS
House Payment	15–30 years	Requires many years of discipline and much money.
Car Payment	2–5 years	Usually a person starts over with the purchase of another vehicle before the first has been completely paid for.
Car Insurance	2–5 years or more	Rarely miss a payment.
Life Insurance	Paid until death.	
Health Insurance	Until death.	
Furniture Payment	Average 2–4 years	Varies, depending upon amount purchased
Utility Bills	Forever	
Country Club Bill	Year-to-year basis	
Telephone Bill	Ongoing	Talk is costly.
Credit Cards	Ongoing	Until paid off or cut up; interest delays payoff date.
Home Rental	Ongoing	Until you move and pay the same, or more, to another landlord.

Building Wealth Using the Tin Can Method

Have you noticed that tithes and offerings didn't make the list due to the fact they aren't paid on a regular basis? Eighty percent of the church don't even factor tithes in, leaving the other 20 percent to pay for the work of all in the church. This is shameful!

Let's get even more realistic. I know the bills on this list are important. All I'm pointing out is the fact that your excuse of not being disciplined enough to save and pay tithes is null and void because of your ability to spend in these places.

> **Think About It—**
> You pay these bills, which means you must have and are displaying some form or type of discipline. And do you know what? Those expenses represent what you want to do and what you don't want to do. They represent where you have chosen to nest and to stockpile your goods. They represent what is important to you.

We pay our life insurance, health insurance, car insurance, house note, house insurance, apartment rent, renter's insurance, and various other things year in and year out for many, many years. Discipline is required in order to pay these bills—discipline, consistency, and respect. In effect, this is how most choose to build their anthills. They respect the people they owe and pay them on time, but they don't respect God and themselves enough to pay Him or themselves consistently on a regular basis. I say *phooey!* If this is you, why do you respect all your bills or obligations more than you do God and yourself? Go to the ant!

> **THINK ABOUT IT—**
> *YOU PAY YOUR LIFE, CAR, HEALTH, AND HOUSEHOLD INSURANCES, HOUSE NOTE OR APARTMENT RENT, AND OTHER THINGS YEAR IN AND YEAR OUT FOR MANY YEARS—SO WHY CAN'T YOU TITHE AND SAVE TOO?*

Let's move on to the next chapter and take a look at one of the most important reasons to establish our finances according to God's biblical order: so that we may live above the failed systems of fallen man and stay out of the destroyer's hands.

Seven
Reasons Not to Trust Man

> Thus saith the LORD; Cursed be the man that trusteth in man, and maketh flesh his arm, and whose heart departeth from the LORD. For he shall be like the heath in the desert, and shall not see when good cometh; but shall inhabit the parched places in the wilderness, in a salt land and not inhabited. Blessed is the man that trusteth in the LORD, and whose hope the LORD is.
> —JEREMIAH 17:5–7

A business magazine I once read stated that figures showed 640 billion dollars were stored away in America's 401(K) tax-deferred retirement plans. The article went on to say that the sums became too appealing to some employers, and they discovered an attractive way to tap into the pot. Because of this "tapping," four hundred of the 270,000 plans were being investigated for possible misuse of funds. Some of these cases were said to have been just plain old stealing.

I'm convinced that Americans must be careful with retirement programs attractively created to lure funds into a holding tank. Sometimes what appears to glitter is not gold, and what man will create for you today may possibly be snatched back tomorrow.

Another example of this is what most Americans have always put their trust in: our infamous social security system. Many people who aren't saving for themselves are quite comfortable in their decision to let social security and other entitlement programs take care of them when their time for retirement comes. They are doing this because of faith in this system. But this is another mistake, because the moneys or trust funds the government can't or won't touch today—they lie in wait for tomorrow. And when man becomes your source, man can let you down.

God said, "Cursed you will be if you put your trust in man [or his financial system], and blessed you will be if you trust in Him [His financial system]." (See Jeremiah 17:5, 7.)

Today we're faced with a social security system and trust fund that aren't managed well enough to meet the needs of upcoming retired Americans. It has really turned out to be a farce. Why? Because there is no real money in these funds, just government IOUs. The government has spent this money. It existed yesterday, but it's gone today. Sure, they will tell you otherwise. They don't want to create a national rebellion, so they repeat half-truths to keep Americans wishing and hoping.

I believe this system needs a higher retirement age and more taxpayers, coupled with higher taxes, to lift itself by the boot straps and replenish the accounts. But even if this were to be enacted, it would not be enough, due to the government's senseless spending and the ever-increasing interest that builds up on government's current debts.

So who bails us out? To whom do we turn? The federal employees retirement system is broke as well. In its vault also sits an IOU. I wonder how many more systems are broke and IOU bound?

Even now, desperation has set into our government, and greed is on the loose like a hungry lion after a drought. The devourer is stalking Washington's halls, and he is hungry. Everything that looks edible will most assuredly be attacked feriously. That's how nearly all government tax-deferred programs, pension funds, retirement accounts, and other entitlement programs are looking right now. No, they won't tell you as of yet, but I certainly would not be surprised if their daily roundtable discussions were seeking masterful means of tapping into these pots. The devourer laid in wait until the appropriate time, and he has pounced on his victims large and small around the American landscape.

I have expressed to friends and colleagues on numerous occasions that I felt tax-deferred company savings programs were created to draw people's money out of their back yard resting places, mattresses, and personal savings accounts in order to help bail out the national debt. Understanding the need for money to deal with the growing debt, I believe the government created many other programs to find another way to generate more money. When has the government really done anything for the American people without having a hidden agenda? *Desperation produces many "unheard-ofs."*

> **THINK ABOUT IT—**
> ANY LAW MAN CREATES TODAY CAN BE RE-CREATED TOMORROW BY THE STROKE OF A PEN. WHY? BECAUSE MAN CAN'T BE TRUSTED.

Don't even mention what's legal and what's illegal, or what's law and what's not—because laws can and will be ignored or disregarded if their inventors feel it is economically expedient to do so. The records and words of some of our leaders confirm this. Remember, "Read my lips, no new taxes"? Of course you do. This statement even helped this leader win election. It was what the American public wanted to hear and trust. But wanting to believe what someone says is one thing, and the politician actually making it good is another.

REASONS NOT TO TRUST MAN

Contracts can and will be broken. Men's words are no longer their bonds. Only God keeps His word. When He says, "I will never leave you or forsake you," you can rest confident in that (Heb. 13:5). God is not a man that He should lie, nor a son of man that He should repent (Num. 23:19). The Bible is His contract to us, and it will never become void or revoked. It hasn't changed in thousands of years. All the promises He made to Abraham were kept, and so were those that were made to us, Abraham's seed. They were good then, and they are good now. So whose report will you believe? For me, I will believe the report of the Lord!

We can no longer trust a system to solve our problems—the system is the problem. Listen to your Creator and follow His financial plan for success, because only He possesses the power to make a difference. You can't trust the report given to you by man or government any longer. I suspect if the American public knew the real deal about our economic situation today, an uprising would occur. Do you honestly think they would want something like that to happen? Of course not. Therefore, I believe the figures and statistics that are revealed to us are a very small fraction of the actual truth.

I also suspect that many who work in these economic departments know what the real picture is like. Everyone is keeping the next department in the dark. No one wants to accept the blame for a lousy job, yet at the same time they desire to keep their jobs. If every government agency corporately brought its true reports to the table, every one of them would probably suffer a heart attack from mere shock!

What I'm angry about, however, is that our government officials have vastly misused the money that we have entrusted into their care. When they've said, "Pay more," we've paid more. When they've said, "Give more," we've given more. When they've said, "Go," we've gone. And when they've said "Stoop," we've stooped. But they have never said *stop,* so we are continuously going and giving. We've been yo-yos long enough. Now they want us to die out so we won't need the squandered retirement funds we've entrusted into their care. (I believe this is why the retirement age is being raised.)

Recall the people in Nehemiah's day. Their situation was much the same as ours today. Today we are faced with the burden of debt, interest, and tax bondage due to our governing laws, and we are being forced to sell our families into slavery, so to speak, through forced multiple jobs to pay our taxes:

> There were also that said, We have borrowed money for the King's tribute and that upon our lands and vineyards. Yet now our flesh is as the flesh of our brethren, our children as their children. And, so, we bring into bondage our sons and daughters to be servants and some of our daughters are brought onto bondage already; neither is it in our power to redeem them; other men have our lands and vineyards.
> —NEHEMIAH 5:4–5

One shouldn't be naive enough to believe honestly that our politicians are going to make the necessary choices to balance our jack rabbit budget! So I caution you again, you can't appease greed. Many of these selfish, greedy governing bodies are corrupting the lives and lifestyles of nearly every American family in this country. For years these politicians have passed the greed baton to themselves and their constituents and are throwing us into an economic collapse of doom and gloom. They lie to get elected or re-elected to fatten their own pockets. They extend their excessive spending habits, overtax us to refund the deficit without changing the system, and then lie, lie, and continue to lie. Remember the cliché: "Figures don't lie...but liars can certainly figure." This cliché represents our government system.

I believe anyone who will continue to put their trust in man can't be dealing with a full deck. God is pulling the curtains off and exposing men's rhetoric so we can get in line with His Word and plan. He wants us to see in what and whom we've been trusting, to expose all their ugliness.

Only God is worthy of our trust, and He has the answers for all humanity:

> Hearken unto me, my people; and give ear unto me, O my nation: for a law shall proceed from me, and I will make my judgment to rest for a light of the people. My righteousness is near; my salvation is gone forth, and mine arms shall judge the people; the isles shall wait upon me, and on mine arm shall they trust.
> —Isaiah 51:4–5

Those who have ears to hear—let them hear!

We Can Reform the Storm

I do believe responsible people can force the corrupt machine in Washington to cease its deception and reform the current storm. They won't do it on their own unless we the people force their hand. For instance, much has been debated about the welfare reform bill. Tens of millions of people were dependent upon it for their welfare and the welfare of their families. Now that is being shaken and revised. For many welfare recipients, their security blanket has been pulled from over their heads. Many recipients of this system became complacent and felt safe, believing the system would always take care of them. Clearly this was a terrible misconception. I can't help but remind these people over and over again, many of whom are Christians, of what the Word of God says, "Put not your trust in man. Cursed be the man who puts his trust in man...blessed be the man who puts his trust in God" (Jer. 17:5, 7). God's Word does

Building Wealth Using the Tin Can Method

not change. He is not a "see-saw" God. He doesn't give and then take back. He is perfect and always means and acts in accordance with what He says. He doesn't make mistakes. And He has a way of bringing people and things into submission. He alone is the almighty God, and our trust and obedience should be only in Him.

I believe there will be more reforms of various laws and statutes, because the American people are slowly waking up. I do believe there are many who truly need welfare assistance. The Word says the poor will always be among us (Matt. 26:11). Many have found themselves thrust into circumstances beyond their control. **However, the good and the needy must often suffer with the bad and the greedy.**

It seems that federal funding for cases of child abuse, domestic violence, and funding for children has been, for the most part, eliminated. Federal guarantees of cash assistance for poor families and children have been compromised. Children from low-income families, pregnant women, the disabled, and nursing home residents will suffer disproportionately. The plan to cut welfare spending by $53 billion dollars over a six-year-period will be felt as a scorpion sting by many.* Deep cuts in Medicare could also hurt many senior citizens—who worked hard by the sweat of their brows to support and build this country. A deep cut could produce many rural hospital closures and reduce the choices many seniors will have. The overall $158 billion cut—$53 billion dollars in the sixth year alone—will most certainly negatively affect senior citizens who are living on fixed incomes.

Where will the extra help needed for these people come from? Who else will be able to assist them? Will you? Are your own finances in order enough to do so?

Medicaid won't be of as much assistance to senior citizens either, since it too will probably suffer deep funding cuts.

Now let's talk a bit about the young, your children and

---

* All welfare and Medicaid figures are based on the article "The 1997 Budget in Review: Who Was Helped? Who Was Hurt?" from the newsletter of Congresswoman Eva M. Clayton, Summer 1996.

mine, who may be adversely affected by the new "educational storm reform" as I call it. It is possible that $200 million dollars may be cut from educational funding. Plans to cap the direct student loan program and the elimination of guaranteed student loans display a nation that is willing to cut its future for its own private selfish benefit. Where is the logic in all of this? Surely Satan is spearheading this nonsense. Right now our governing leaders are puppets on his string.

Fools are rushing in where wise men dare not tread. The United States government today has eyes that can't see and ears that can't hear. Much of what is being done in Washington isn't for the betterment of we the American people, nor is it for the balancing of the budget. If their program cuts were truly intended toward that end, why would they propose to borrow money for the purpose of giving tax breaks to the wealthiest Americans?[*] Where is the shared sacrifice? Why have we the people allowed this nonsense to go on for so long to the point that the "powers that be" now view us as blind bats? We gave them carte blanche over the years to rob our paychecks and write hot checks; all of this simply must stop.

I believe the resulting ricochet from the axing of all of these government programs will eventually produce a monstrosity of economic earthquakes that will rock this world. It's a sure guarantee. Millions of people, especially children, will be ghastly affected. I believe child abuse will rise to unheard of proportions. Victims of domestic violence will surely increase with no one or no program to help. Funeral parlors will make even more money due to increased "body" business.

Many government officials travel in limousines paid for with our tax dollars while mothers and children are being hacked to death by irate, out-of-work fathers who are constantly being denied a job. Why isn't a program developed whereby each member of a governing body takes one

---

[*] From the Summer 1996 newsletter of Congresswoman Eva M. Clayton

Building Wealth Using the Tin Can Method

family into its sprawling home and assists these hardship cases until that family can fare better? This is just a suggestion!

But while they are under your roof, Senator, why don't you use some of your contacts to find a job for them? Better still, share your salary with them. There's more than enough food in your many freezers, and your maids could cook and wash for them as well. After all, your five or more guest rooms would be more than adequate to house them for a while. You can afford it! Just downsize some of your spending. Eliminate a vacation to Switzerland or one of the monthly social gatherings where you show off before your peers. I'm sure there's many other areas not mentioned that you could curtail as well. Don't worry about what it will cost you. We the people have been paying for it anyway with our taxes. You wouldn't lose anything except your image, I suppose. But you can afford to lose that. It will be good for you. Maybe these new house guests could also tell you, in detail, about the real world.

And what will you do, Congressman, when the elderly start to suffer more abuse due to a lack of adequate care? Rather than go through such anguish, many will die from loneliness and hopelessness. Education for many will be too much of a task for which to find funding, so it will get lost in the "not-worth-the-pain-or-strain" column.

Yes, a storm from the reform. Who or where will be our "great white hope"? Surely, if there is such a person or thing, the need to show up is now.

To me it is funny while heartbreakingly pathetic that eagles, sea animals, leaves, plastic, and all kinds of environmental "stuff" seem to receive top priority in the hearts and minds of Americans today. Millions of dollars are being raked up to study and protect these so-called valuable endangered species. I thought our own human species was supposed to be more valuable than anything else. But man's priorities are warped. Men's minds have become seduced, bewitched, and controlled by the devil himself.

I could go on and on about the negatives that surrounds these issues. But what we need are solutions. And the solutions are not in man, they are in God.

> The fool hath said in his heart, There is no God. They are corrupt, they have done abominable works, there is none that doeth good.
> —PSALM 14:1

Remember that God sits very high and looks low. He's no fool. Those in Washington who say in their heart, "There is no God," and play little gods over us are the fools. God is our loving Creator who judges with a strong hand. Nothing escapes Him.

Yet again I say to the masses of people—we are to blame. We, the people, must return and embrace God, our Father. Then we must seize the opportunity to hold accountable and put into office those honorable citizens who are worthy and fit. There are many who understand their human condition and respect the things of God. We have the opportunity and the power to vote and change the outcome. We have the power to reform the storm.

Today, God is calling. He is pleading with America to return to Him so He can return to us. He desires to heal our wounds and restore our land. **But we must get in order.** We must reverence and obey His written and accurate instructions. He is looking for *Calebs* and *Joshuas* who believe they are more than able to conquer the land despite the presence of giants (Num. 13:30). Even today, with God we can master anything.

You can't look to the system. Stop believing in man's economy and way of doing things! Man's system can change midstream at any time and at any place without warning. We can't afford to pull our hands out of God's hands! We must learn to cultivate a relationship of trust in the God who can deliver solutions. It is relationship with God, not with Satan's failed world systems, that we must seek to improve and invest in. When righteous men and women replace those who are squandering America's future (through free and open elections), the people will rejoice, because righteousness exalts any nation that submits itself to God.

> Blessed be the man who puts his trust in God...cursed be the man who puts his trust in man.
> —Jeremiah 17:5, 7

Corporate America Needs a Corporate God

> Righteousness exalteth a nation: but sin is a reproach to any people.
> —Proverbs 14:34

Another reason not to trust man is the job insecurity that greedy downsizing has produced over the past few years. Today's standard of living has reached an all-time high. Many have played the volatile stock market and hit it big. The salaries of many CEOs are steadily inflating. Many are displaying their wealth through the purchase of expensive automobiles and the building of elaborate homes. Huge malls have become the entertainment center for the family. Vacations have become more frequent and lavish. The sky's the limit! Nothing is wrong with any of these nice things—except when we put more trust in things than we do in God.

On the opposite end of the spectrum is another segment of citizens whose standard of living is declining. Many corporate Americans are no longer making their once-large salaries and drinking coffee in their swank offices because of the downsizing that has been occurring. Many are finding themselves job-hunting again, and in many cases they are having to settle for a much lower salary to keep food on their tables. Many have been caught unaware because they thought their jobs were secure. And because they were caught unaware, they had made little or no financial provision for their unexpected termination.

Many white *and* blue collar workers had hoped their seniority within their companies and corporations would keep them there. These people most assuredly depended upon the high salaries and pensions created for them by these companies.

> **THINK ABOUT IT—**
> WE MUST ALWAYS REMEMBER THAT WHAT MAN CREATED AND PROMISED YOU TODAY—HE CAN RE-CREATE AND RENEGE ON TOMORROW.

Corporate downsizing today will continue to rob many incomes. And poverty is on the rise, even though we have high employment. Crime and drugs are rampant in America's neighborhoods, regardless of income levels and locations.

Our government has been losing the battle to deal with crime effectively. Racism and hate is on a national rise. The American economy is facing impending collapse of entitlement programs. Our medical care system is expensive and inadequate. The grotesque indebtedness of our government is fueling a ghastly feeling of cynicism and hopelessness.

Our children demonstrate an attitude of indecisiveness, irresponsibility, and licentiousness. The destinies of many babies are being denied through abortion. Powerful special interest groups fund and support unimportant issues as long as the focus is detoured from issues that may threaten their pockets. No longer is truth and integrity criteria for electing governing candidates.

We must depend upon God. As we do, He will *return*

unto us, heal our land, and deliver us from destruction. We must *return* to the values and ethics that are attributed to making this nation great and strong. In God our forefathers trusted, and in God we must trust again.

Corporate America needs a corporate God. No one can expect companies to make adequate provision or to put aside savings for them. Why should they? That's not their responsibility. It's your responsibility, and it always has been. **No one is going to look out for your financial well-being better than yourself.** You can't put your trust in man or his system. Remember what Jeremiah said: "Blessed be the man who puts his trust in God [and]...cursed be the man who puts his trust in man."

Many gray-haired people who have put their trust in man can be found in "outplacement seminars" around the country. Layoffs are affecting older workers the most. Today many companies are deciding they no longer need their numerous middle managers, many who happen to be forty or older. Why? Older workers tend to be paid more, and greed is taking its toll. Can you imagine working faithfully for a company for twenty-three years only to be fired because of your high salary? God knows the limitations and fallacies of man all too well. That's why He explicitly tells us to put no trust in any man. We pay dearly when we disregard God's Word and look to man.

God is a jealous God, and the Word clearly states, "Thou shall have no other gods before Me." This includes the "gods" many companies have made themselves out to be. Many are finding out the hard way that God—not man—is their source. Deuteronomy 18:18 says, "It is He who gives you the power to get wealth," not you or your company! The earth is the Lord's and the fullness thereof, and all that dwells within it. God owns the cattle upon a thousand hills. He is omniscient and omnipresent. In other words, God sees everything, owns everything, and is everywhere. So in whose plan should we trust and invest? Shouldn't it be the one who truly owns it all and who has a proven track record?

You can't continue to trust in entities that are just as guilty as you are in financial matters.

THINK ABOUT IT—
THEY CAN'T HELP YOU WHEN THEY ARE PRESSING YOU SEVERELY TO HELP THEM.

Just as when you read a sign on a soda machine that says *Out of Order,* so is this country. Everything is out of order. It doesn't matter how many quarters you put into an out-of-order soda machine. You can plop in five dollars' worth, and you still won't get a soda. *Out of order* means "broken, nonfunctioning, in need of repair"—and we have been putting millions of dollars in quarters into Satan's greed machine, without getting our promised return.

When even more companies begin to downsize, who do you think they will eliminate, or whose salary will they cut first? Certainly not their own! They have their image and lifestyles to maintain as well. They will cut you, and you'll be left out to fare for yourselves because the company that said you'd be working for them until retirement suddenly pulled the rug out from under you! Now your wife, who had the option of working or not, will have to join the work force. The nice things to which you had become accustomed will become a passing memory. Your pension will have been completely robbed or tremendously depleted, especially after taxes.

Downsizing is a curse derived from man's disobedience. It is the result of godless, selfish planning that gives no consideration to God—and it is causing many to fall. Corporate America needs a corporate God, and God is calling. The time is long past when any plan of man's will work financially for our benefit! *I believe God is allowing us* *to see, through the numerous past, present, and future greedy disasters, that His plan of provision is the only thing that is certain.*

Should a few individuals who control and benefit from all the billions being pulled in by these corporations be allowed to maintain their jobs, while millions of other hard workers are out there hurting? Will you opt to get in order? Or will you continue trusting man and suffer until a greater evil befalls you?

Listen Christians, this country has no business being run by the majority of the people who are running it now. They don't qualify. What makes matters even worse is that most of us aren't qualified, either. Why? Because we haven't executed our rightful positions in all matters concerning mankind as God has intended. This includes physical, spiritual, and financial matters.

Man's plan will forsake you, but God never will. What He says is what He means, and He always delivers on His promise. When we get in order with God's biblical plan, we can look forward to His rebuking this stalking devourer. He will catch the thief and cause him to restore unto us seven times what has been stolen. God is saying if we return unto Him, He will mostly assuredly return unto us.

It's Time to Start Over Again!

Let God pick you up by your bootstraps and start all over again. This time, start with a plan that has been tried, proven, and tested for thousands of years. There is proof that no person has ever lost a dime. Prosperity and family security are the tested fruit of God's righteous way. As David proclaimed in Psalm 37:25, "I have been young, and now am old; yet have I not seen the righteous forsaken, nor his seed begging bread."

This generation hasn't been smart enough to save; therefore it doesn't have much. But God knows how to get our attention. Who will cover you when it's time for you to retire? If you can't provide for yourself, who will?

There are many who are trying to recover what the thief has stolen, and in many cases they are making a fantastic difference. Praise God for that! However, many of us aren't listening and have fallen short of becoming the army we should be—collectively and corporately. We should be taking the world by storm. When there's a battle or uprising, the army of God should always be arrayed and ready to fight and win!

There are all types of negative financial predictions and speculations coming out of the secular world, telling us to brace ourselves for the worst, more now than ever before. **This is why the government and businesses have been battling over your small change.** There is a deadly and destructive cloud hovering over this nation in the area of finances. This monster is no joke, and it is playing for keeps! Out of your hands into theirs—this is their financial plan. So wake up and fight! We must get back to appreciating the value of our pennies, nickels, and dimes. **Use them, and build your own wealth.** We must show those who are in darkness the marvelous light. They don't know the way out. Unless we show them the way, they will be led astray. God's Word says, "I am the way, the truth, and the life" (John 14:6).

The tin can message is one of simplicity that even a child can understand. No strange speech or hard language. It is a message of what God can do in times of adversity—and when times are good. It is a message of wisdom and preparation. And it is a message of God's tremendous love.

Remember, our change—pennies, nickels, dimes, and quarters—add up to thousands of dollars when we stay in God's order and learn to save. As we put God first with His tithes and offerings, then pay our tin can, He will give the increase. And regardless of how the powers that be try to take our money, we will stand financially free. Those who

BUILDING WEALTH USING THE TIN CAN METHOD

have ears, let them hear!

THINK ABOUT IT—
SMALL CHANGE DOES ADD UP AND MAKE HUGE SUMS OF MONEY!

Now get ready to take an inside look at the banking industry's contributions to the financial crises of our day through their greedy practices of usury, which is robbing you of the chance to build your wealth.

Eight

Interest From Hell

Since the Fed is the only "legal entity" that can create money, if, as an example, it lends to you $100 at 7 percent interest, at the end of one year, you would owe $107. Where will you get the extra seven dollars, except borrow it?

Usury, or *interest,* is one the most controversial concepts in economics. It came into widespread use in various European countries near the latter part of the sixteenth century. Before then, the receiving of interest on loans had long been considered contrary to divine law; it was regarded as the sin of usury.* It has been attacked as degrading to the human spirit and corrosive upon the foundations of society.

The love of filthy lucre—or the pursuit of money by the greedy through unjust terms and means—is detested by God (1 Tim. 3:3). Money is by no means regarded as sin or evil, but it is irreversibly regarded as filthy when its gain is connected to the kind of usury that historically produced hardships and even imprisonment in debtor's prisons.

The Hebrew term for *usury* or *interest* is *neshek,* which literally means, "a bite." But in Jeremiah 8:17 it is also used as to mean "a serpent's bite." How more accurate could this be? Interest is a bite—a huge one for the debtor. This is what actually takes place in our finances every time we are charged usury on anything we purchase. Of course, you

---

* *The New Palgrave Dictionary of Economics,* vol. 2, page 882.

and I both know that anything that bites also hurts, and in some instances kills.

Nehemiah had to rebuke his own people for exacting usury or interest that thrust their Hebrew brothers into debt (Neh. 5:7). The usury or interest rate on the average credit card today hovers around 18 percent. This actually qualifies as a form of collective insanity. For example, anyone who charges a big-screen TV that costs $1,500 at 18 percent usury rate and pays only the minimum due each month will pay around $1,673 in interest over the twelve years it would take to pay off.

I'm convinced that the indebtedness of many is due to their own abuse and misuse of their money. However, I also believe that usury is another financial form that has robbed thousands of people of their savings and potential savings. Many savings plans have been depleted or never started because of debts owed to pay the average percentage charged for various services!

A Satanic Rig

It is difficult to get ahead when the amount of an item purchased is running rampant with interest charges. The first item purchased gets paid for once, and the interest being charged pays for the item again, and then some. This causes other problems, such as the purchase of other necessary items or the hazard of ruined credit histories. The money that might have been available in a household for the purchase of other needed items is being absorbed by usury on the first item.

Let's look at one of the biggest purchases most people make during their life—their home. Millions of people are in debt in this country because of what they owe on their homes. Do you realize that the majority of these people have already paid in full for the cost of that home? Most should have had a mortgage-burning ceremony years ago.

But because of the excessive interest imposed by the lending institutions, they are paying for their homes two and three times over.

One could pay for a $200,000 house and still have a savings of $200,000 or more within a decent number of years if it weren't for usury. A $200,000 house with a 10 percent interest or usury rate for thirty years will cost you about $600,000 or more.

It is relatively easy to pay for most things the first time around, especially if the item purchased is within one's financial means or capability. But while you're paying for that item, additional maintenance or upkeep costs must also be paid.

Let's imagine a bit here. After making enough mortgage payments to have paid for a home the first time around, let's say that only a minimal amount of upkeep was needed, and you were able to manage these costs also. But a number of years have passed since your purchase, and now your property is older. Things you didn't have to do ten years ago to maintain the home are now required. Although you paid enough to pay for the house once, remember you must continue to juggle and make mortgage payments, paying for it a second time—along with more frequent maintenance costs. And remember, the second and third time around you are merely paying interest.

Let's also say that your job hasn't given you adequate pay raises to balance out these rising costs. Now you're falling behind on the house taxes because the interest rate is running like a jack rabbit, which is almost impossible to catch unless a miracle comes your way.

Also consider the enormous downsizing of the deductions you're being allowed to take today on your taxes. What you could have deducted last year is far smaller this year in order to make more money for the government and less for you. That $500 payment that you must now pay in interest could very well have been tucked away as a yearly

BUILDING WEALTH USING THE TIN CAN METHOD

savings for your family. But now it's gone just by the stroke of a pen, by a law.

Maybe the expenses for your family of four increased through various unexpected medical bills. Now as you file your taxes (because of the various changes in deductions), you find yourself owing a tax amount you just can't afford to pay—but could have paid if your continuous house-interest obligation had not absorbed it. Tax penalties kick in as a result, so you make arrangements to pay installments. But you're still not able to get a grip on your finances because of the difficult year you had with illness and a couple of installment tax payments. The excessive interest (more than 24 percent) for your tax payments is accruing daily, until the entire amount is due because of default. Bam! Now you're in debt due to unexpected causes from the year. You try to explain your situation to the lending institution, and they either threaten to foreclose on your property or put a lien on it, depending on the balance owed on your mortgage.

Meanwhile, interest is still accruing, so the mortgage holder suggests you get another loan—which will require more debt. The tax people threaten to garnish your check. This will undoubtedly cause a series of catastrophes, because other necessary obligations for your family won't be financially fulfilled due to the garnished wages. Now you may be faced with bad credit and humiliating court appearances for failure to pay your bills.

Tension begins to mount in your family. Your entire life—and the American dream—is down the tube, thanks to the demon called *usury*. You're a prime candidate for Satan's suggestions to take your life or destroy your family. Get the picture? How's this for a frightening imagination? Yes, imposed upon one brother or fellowman by another—and supported by the system.

People everywhere today are crying, "Get out of debt; get out of debt!" But it's down right impossible in many cases because of the constant and consistent imposing of fees, surcharges, and interest. You can't control your indebtedness when someone is saying "Not yet, you're not finished; you owe me two more times." It's impossible!

The bite of the usury lender can really hurt and sometimes kill. This is why God said, "Take thou no usury of him, or increase: but fear thy God; that thy brother may live with thee. Thou shalt not give him thy money upon usury, nor lend him thy victuals for increase" (Lev. 25:36–37).

The Hebrew word *increase* here is *marbit* or *tarbit,* which means "the multiplication or gain of the creditor due to accrued interest." Now here is some truth from God's Word that will probably shake many to the core of their being. According to Ezekiel 18:8–17, lending on usury or increase is condemned with a sentence of death. It is listed among the worst of sins or gravest of crimes. Why? Because of the financial burden it can impose. This nation and its citizens are in great debt because of interest. It is for this reason that I personally believe usury is worthy of being outlawed because of its influence in producing social ruin.

WORTHY OF DEATH

In Ezekiel, usury is mentioned along with adultery, homicide, larceny, and other similar "abominations" that are worthy of death.

> Hath given forth upon usury, and hath taken increase: shall he then live? he shall not live: he hath done all these abominations; he shall surely die; his blood shall be upon him.
> —EZEKIEL 18:13

Psalm 15:5 proclaims the rejection of usury in lending practices as one of the positive attributes of a righteous man.

Building Wealth Using the Tin Can Method

> He that putteth not out his money to usury, nor taketh reward against the innocent. He that doeth these things shall never be moved.
> —Psalm 15:4–5

The augmentation of substance by interest and increase is listed among the "evil men" in Proverbs 28:8.

> He that by usury and unjust gain increaseth his substance, he shall gather it for him that will pity the poor.
> —Proverbs 28:8

God has warned mankind for thousands of years on the prohibitions of this sin. If you didn't know it before, you certainly know it now. In His omniscience, God knows the negative consequences that each sin can produce in our lives. So He left us *warnings, woes, lest you's, take heeds,* and *thou shalt nots* to which we are to give special attention and careful consideration so as to avoid certain pitfalls. Now you are held accountable to see that God has warned and forbidden us to participate in *usury*.

THINK ABOUT IT—
IN EZEKIEL 18:13, LENDING ON USURY OR INCREASE IS CLASSED AMONG THE WORST OF SINS.

> And has charged interest or percentage of increase on what he has loaned [in supposed compassion] shall he then live. He shall not live. He has done all these abominations, he shall surely die His blood shall be upon him.
> —AMP

Conversely, Ezekiel 18:17 says:

> Who has withdrawn his hand from pressing the poor who has not received interest or increase [from the needy] but has executed my ordinances, and has walked in my statues; he shall not die for the iniquity of his father; he shall surely live.
>
> —AMP

God knew that satanically inspired men would find a way to get rich off the weak, poor, desperate, and needy, so He warned against and condemned usury. God knew all too well that usury would lie at the root of social and economic ruin for man. Many people young and old have committed suicide, fled the country, lost their health and savings, and are now living below the poverty level because of the excessive usury that has been thrust upon them by the world system. Interest today is being charged and accrued on almost every service that is being provided.

Whom can the American citizen consult to halt these demonic rates? Our government? Most certainly not! It's the culprit as well—the biggest of them! It is woefully out of control. Our national debt with its rising interest could easily cause anyone to throw in the towel. Our government can't pay off its own debts, and neither can we.

Morals and ethics have escaped our leaders. Their theme has become, "Let me get mine before the bottom falls all the way out." Many citizens are enslaved and living in the bondage of a modern-day Egypt because of the debt put upon them by the rules, regulations, and laws of a sick, out-of-control, greedy system. Hundreds of billions of dollars that could be helping the poor are being wasted yearly by our government.

Potential savings money is being taken away from citizens in taxes. Bureaucratic rhetoric and nonsense peeks out from it's selfish comfort zone to rule with disgust and inhumane methods. We try to follow and submit to their wavering rules while hoping to never be the recipient of

Building Wealth Using the Tin Can Method

one of their audits. We're forced to work hundreds of hours a year just to keep financial records and fill out "mumble-jumble." Many times the forms are too complicated to read—they are devised by the devil. What tax auditors look for and find could cost you thousands of dollars by the time they slap you with their penalties, which is interest, fines (which are also interest!), and the interest on top of that interest. Interest, interest, interest!

Many have been forced to borrow, with interest of course, from their local lending "interest institutions" to pay off their ever-accruing tax bills of interest. Surely this is what God was condemning in Ezekiel. Honesty means nothing and plays no part with this agency backed by our government. Recent IRS hearings have shown that the people are speaking up, but there is so much more speaking we have to do! You work hard, you raise your family, you obey the law, yet they seek honest mistakes and oversights to feed their greed by putting liens on the properties of law-abiding citizens, freezing their bank accounts, and garnishing their pay checks. And your "friendly" banks where you put your money are stealing on the other end and are increasing their profits. It's called friendships and kinships.

Yet, what would America be without you and me as citizens? Should we, as supposedly free people, live this way? First John 4:18 says that "fear hath torment," and many Americans are living day to day in fear of their own government, which is supposed to be working for "we the people." With this ongoing nonsense, how can "we the people" leave an inheritance to our children's children to finance and enhance the gospel?

Legalized Thieves!

Listen to me, you workers of iniquity—you have invented legalized stealing, and God will not stand for it. Recent public uproar is just the tip of the iceberg. There is a justice and law above yours that condemns your actions! You will not escape! Some of the insane interest rates you charge cannot be paid at the rate at which they are accruing. Many people can't even make the kind of money that you are assessing in usury and fines. Many work for minimum wages; yet they are harassed to pay your 20 to 40 percent tax and interest rates! It's financial apartheid.

Financial death and physical death are very close cousins. Take your choice—either one will lay you in a coffin. We the people built this country by the sweat of our brows. Yet you, the government of the country we've built and supported, are robbing us blind. Repent!

A WORD OF ENCOURAGEMENT TO THE FAITHFUL

God will bring a wave of supernatural debt cancellation for the obedient who are in order. The governmental and lending institution debt that hover over many consists of excessive interest, fees, and taxes—and is pure sin. It is forbidden in God's written law. God knew Satan would inspire men to seize the moment and cause human ruin. The interest of today's financial systems stands behind anything man does, and he justifies his human actions with it. "Well, you see, you must pay, because, after all, it is the law..."

So omniscient God was right "on the money" when He said, "[If a man] hath not given forth upon usury, neither hath taken any increase, that hath withdrawn his hand from iniquity, hath executed true judgment between man and man...to deal truly; he is just, he shall surely live, saith the Lord GOD.... [But if he has] given forth upon usury, and hath taken increase...he shall not live: he hath done all these abominations; he shall surely die; his blood shall be upon him" (Ezek. 18:8–9, 13).

This prohibition from taking interest was obviously a problem in biblical times. In Ezekiel 22:12, the prophet judged those who had "taken interest and increase" as those who had forgotten God.

> In thee have they taken gifts to shed blood; thou hast taken usury and increase, and thou hast greedily gained of thy neighbours by extortion, and hast forgotten me, saith the Lord God.
> —Ezekiel 22:12

By whatever it does, each generation affects those who come after it. Today mankind has seized the moment to create an "interest hell" for our children. Today's youth will surely bring charges against us because of our current financial situation. They certainly don't want to foot the bill for the ineptitude of those who were before them. God will personally deal with the individuals who created this mess. No one who is guilty will escape. The actions of any one person can profoundly affect numerous others. There is a cause-and-effect situation here. Remember the Achan principle? What one chooses to do can infect another with disease, prejudice his mind, and generally tip the scales in favor of evil. We are makers of destiny for one another. Therefore, the importance of treading carefully and obeying God's Word is important. God doesn't hold a man responsible for the circumstances into which he was born, but He will hold him responsible for what he does within those circumstances.

So I say again to you, men of evil, don't persuade yourself to believe that your fortunes will remain as though you were God instead of mere men. God's divine judgment will go forward regardless of any fantasies that you may hold dear. Outside your gold-plated houses, the poor whom you are oppressing are crying to God for justice, and He will answer. Mary's prophecy in Luke 1:52–53 puts it in a most poetic tone: "He hath put down the mighty from their seats, and exalted them of low degree. He hath filled the hungry with good things; and the rich he hath sent empty away."

The evil destroyers of men through unjust interest will face their day of reckoning:

> He that by usury and unjust gain increaseth his substance, he shall gather it for him that will pity the poor.
> —Proverbs 28:8

> He that putteth not out his money to usury, nor taketh reward against the innocent. He that doeth these things shall never be moved.
> —Psalm 15:5

> And all the trees of the field shall know—understand and realize—that I, the Lord, have brought low the high tree, have exalted the low tree, have dried up the green tree, and have made the dry tree flourish. I the Lord, have spoken, and *I will do it.*
> —Ezekiel 17:24, AMP, EMPHASIS ADDED

God is a "reverser of the fortunes" of men. He is an even and fair distributor. Who can stand before Him? What can be done?

> Because he considereth, and turneth away from all his transgression that he hath committed he shall surely live, he shall not die.
> —Ezekiel 18:28

Those who represent us (our elected officials) should not have approved the senseless powers that, if continued, may well destroy mankind. But I believe God's hands are stayed for the moment to allow repentance for everyone—including you, powers that be—to get back into God's divine order. *God's mercy always calls out for man's repentance.* Even after years of wrongdoing, all men can be brought into a new relationship with God and turn to good.

You who are currently oppressing this nation through your own unjust gain—you don't have to die. Certainly it would bring no pleasure to God. Every human being possesses the power to change their past into a beautiful future for themselves and for their children. That's the duty for which we were created. As we accept the sacrifice of Jesus Christ, who died in our stead to pay the penalty for sin, God does not judge us for what we were, but rather for what we presently are—new creations in Christ. This defines the gospel, for surely God's mercy is good news. We're made in His image. He loves us. He fashioned us all, the good and the bad. As Ezekiel invited the unrighteous of his day, God's Word invites the unrighteous of our own:

> Cast away from you all the transgressions which you have committed against me, and get yourselves a new heart and a new spirit: why will you die, O house of Israel?
> —Ezekiel 19:31

So He is appealing to you today, in this book:

> Because he considereth and turneth away from all his transgression that he hath committed, he shall surely live, he shall not die.
> —Ezekiel 18:28

> That if thou shalt confess with thy mouth the Lord Jesus, and shalt believe in thine heart that God hath raised him from the dead, thou shalt be saved.
> —Romans 10:9

The evil powers that be will step down by the sovereign hand of God. He has decreed it!

I will overthrow, overthrow, overthrow it; this shall be no more until He comes whose right it is to reign in judgment and in righteousness and I will give it to Him.

—Ezekiel 21:27, AMP

But you, O rich man, need not suffer this. Repent now, and receive God's grace. Any injustice between a man and his fellowman will weaken the fabric of any society and create or set in motion its destruction. *The issue of usury is certainly necessary for all to face. It must not be propounded. Interest is a huge tin can robber!*

In the next chapter I will help you to understand much of the fine print in the bank papers that you have probably never read. What it says—and the power it gives—has been making the unrighteous rich.

NINE
FEES FROM HELL

If the American people allow private banks to control the issuance of their currency, first by inflation and then by deflation, the banks and corporations that grow up around them will deprive the people of all their property, until their children will wake up homeless on the continent their fathers conquered.

—THOMAS JEFFERSON

Nearly a thousand U.S. banks, including savings and loans, defaulted in the late 1980s and early 1990s. The estimated cost of these highly publicized savings and loan bailouts was a whopping $550 billion plus. It is said that the cost of the Vietnam War didn't come close to matching this figure. As a matter of fact, the bailout was over twelve times the cost of the war. How did these financial institutions get themselves into such a mess? Risky business—big time risky business! Their bad decisions and investments cost American taxpayers billions and billions of dollars. Do you think either you or I will ever get the chance to risk their money like that? Of course not! It's complicated just to get a loan. To many banks, loaning their money is risky business.

Nevertheless, the FDIC bailed them out *with taxpayer money.* The bailout caused the FDIC fund to diminish rapidly, requiring an abundance of additional funding to

FEES FROM HELL

remain alive. As a matter of fact, during that time the FDIC funds were so depleted that Congress immediately had to step in to rescue them by providing emergency funding. (But where did this emergency funding come from? We the taxpayers! We the people paid this hefty bill, whether you realized it or not.) In 1993 the Federal Government estimated that FDIC losses (losses of we the people) were somewhere near $70 billion.*

Where will the funds come from should there be a "next time," and who will come to their rescue or aid? I pray that the FDIC will avoid the same problem if it ever arises again, because we the taxpayers are already paying exorbitant amounts of money for our own personal bailouts and high taxes; we can't withstand much more. No question about it!

STUPENDOUS BAILOUTS

Since the FDIC's stupendous bailouts, our personal financial situations have also suffered. At that time there were more than nine hundred FDIC "problem banks" with assets that exceeded more than half a trillion dollars. In total, 744 banks were closed or sold during the crisis that began in 1989. It impacted twenty-five million depositors and involved $219 billion dollars in assets that were put at risk.* It has been said that because of this, many U. S. banks will remain problematic into the twenty-first century. This means depositors who have $100,000 or more in a bank will often need to check up intelligently on the financial health of the institution that is holding their funds.

Even though the FDIC is purported to be healthy again today and a calmness has seemed to set in, my question to you is, "Could this happen again under a new set of circumstances?" Not everyone learns from their mistakes, especially when they are at the expense of others. If our fathering government hasn't been able to balance the national budget after all these years, what can one hope or expect from its

---

*Based on figures from the *Chase Investment Performance Digest: Performance and Rankings of the World's Major Investments,* 1960–1996 (Concord, MA: Chase Global Data and Research), 1997.

dependent children? We, the American people, are the ones who have been paying for the lousy, irresponsible habits of these banking institutions. But after paying for their rehabilitation via Congress, they have become even more greedy. **They have become adverse fee creators.** This is how they repaid the people for bailing them out. Taxpayers paid for their lousy lack of wisdom, and their way of saying "thank you" has been to charge us excessive fees. I believe their inept failures led them to seek a way to recoup their losses, so they put on their unscrupulous thinking caps and reasoned out a manipulative way to put themselves back on top of the crisis through fees—fees from hell.

We the people are constantly paying for other institutions' errors when the powers that be make mistakes. It's a fairly easy job to make a mistake and have someone else pick up the tab for it. But aren't you tired of picking up the tabs for affairs you had no say in and weren't even invited to participate in? I recall Jesse Jackson speaking out on a political issue, saying, "I didn't attend the party, I wasn't invited to the party, so why should I have to pay for the party?" These are my sentiments exactly concerning these bailouts.

When government and big business make senseless mistakes, we the people are forcibly invited to pick up the "big spender's" tab. This happens more than you would truly want to know, and it brings us back to what I have been saying all along. But who is willing to pick up our tab? We're heavily penalized and even jailed in necessary for making mistakes. *So you see, we can't afford not to obey God.* We must follow God's laws, rules, principles, and guidelines. These people are literally burning the money for which we labored. The scales aren't balanced, but they need to be. People who try to obey the system are constantly getting burned by that system.

Our parents and foreparents have been raped of the privileges owed them. They have been financially punished for doing what they were told. The elderly have been pushed

FEES FROM HELL

aside, unappreciated, and forgotten—and so will we. Our government has displayed a selfishness and unconcern for others. An increasing number of Americans live at or near the poverty level. According to the Senate Committee on Aging, there are as many elderly who are deemed poor as the nonelderly today; an even larger portion of elderly are living in "near poverty" status. One of the reasons for this trend is the fact that there are more people reaching the ranks of the elderly today than ever before. For example, our nation's medium age in 1992 was 33. Today it is 36. But by the year 2030, it is estimated that the average age will be age 42.* By the end of a baby boomer's natural lifetime, it is said that there could be two retirees for every teenager.

In light of these statistics, I believe the *fees* the banks so lucratively have collected could more than take care of this nation's elderly. Banks across this country are reporting major profit gains from fees.** So surely they can more than afford to assist the nation's elderly. This could be a pet project for them to redeem themselves and give back a portion of what they have taken from American taxpayers. But do you think they will? Of course not! They are after the elderly's money too, even if they do offer so-called "Golden Years" accounts. In some way, form, or fashion, they are going to collect a fee from them, even if it's just fifty cents.

BIG PROFITS!

Fees are big profit makers for banks and other institutions and businesses. I was having dinner at a restaurant not long ago when a television report aired that discussed various branch banks that were going to phase out a number of their employees over the next five years. It was stated that computerized money machines would replace their "people employees." Machines would now be handling many banking services for customers that were once handled by

---

*Based on figures from the *Chase Investment Performance Digest: Performance and Rankings of the World's Major Investments,* 1960–1996 (Concord, MA: Chase Global Data and Research), 1997.

** *The Raleigh News and Observer,* July 16, 1996.

people. It was at that moment that the Spirit of the Lord allowed me to see that the whole purpose for this transition was for lending institutions to justify charging higher fees, even though banks already have managed to "legally" fee its customers into frenzies.

A newspaper article I read some time ago reported on the fee profits of two of North Carolina's largest banks.* I'm sure the same is true of other banks across this country. It stated that the customers were angry about erroneous fee charges. The article said one of the banks in question reported $605 million in earnings for a consecutive three-month period in 1996. I'm sure that amount is much higher today. Think About It: a huge percentage of that $605 million is *free*...oh, I mean *fee* money. Believe me, it's one and the same. This amount was said to be a 30 percent increase from the same period the year before. Of course, each year they created new terminology for new fees. The second bank reported $439 million in earnings with a 21 percent increase. A banking consultant was quoted as saying that fees were the fuel that had driven the increases. For the past seven years, banks have been seeing record profits, and along with the growing profits have also come growing fees.

IT'S TIME TO GET ANGRY

The problem with many long overdue ills in this country is that we the people seem to get angry about many areas of ridiculous government and business practices for only a short period. Then we accept them, absorb them, and go on. So our government and the other powers that be have become accustomed to our repetitious adjustments and know just when to pull another one on us. Maybe if we would learn to maintain our dissatisfaction with unfair practices, things would change.

I began to speak out years ago to my customers, family, and friends about fees. At that time, they were not close to

---
* Joel B. Obermayer, "Fee increases pay off in profits for N.C. banks," *Raleigh News and Observer*, July 16, 1996.

the amount being charged today. I remember when NSF (nonsufficient funds) charges were five dollars. Today, although it varies across the country, some banks charge thirty dollars or more. NSF charges initially were supposedly implemented to deter bad-check writers. But I am convinced this was an untruth from the beginning. The same bad-check writers are still around doing the same things, and the judicial system isn't harsh enough on them even when they're caught. Jails and prisons "need room" for worse offenders, so bad-check writers get released and commit the same crimes over and over again. This gives the banks a justifiable reason to increase the fee, which, by the way, increases their profits. Thus, banks promote steadily rising increases in order to weed out the bad guys—while at the same time they hope that the bad guys will increase.

Legalized Crooks

The intentional bad-check writers and erroneous-fee chargers are one and the same to me. Either way you look at it, they both are out to get you. The only difference is that if one group gets caught, they're prosecuted, but the other group never goes to court. How can you win? Only God can, and will, even this score.

This fee frenzy has been taking money that could have been put in savings accounts. Wicked banks and other entities that have been profiting unjustly won't have the last laugh, because Proverbs 28:8 says, "He who increases his wealth by exorbitant interest amasses it for another, who will be kind to the poor" (NIV). In other words, God will insure that the wealth of the wicked is laid up for the righteous. Supernatural redirecting of these funds is coming in the last days. Those who are in order will be the recipients.

My sister and some others now look at me in awe, remembering those years when the Lord prompted me in 1992 to predict that our nation's fee craze would get out of control. I

Building Wealth Using the Tin Can Method

told them it would be because of greed and our acceptance of it that these fees would increase. Back then as I rattled off what God was allowing me to foresee, I'm sure many felt that I had fallen off the deep end and was being too emotional, because twenty-five and fifty-cent fees were common at that time. To them, that was insignificant chunk change. Why buck the system? But even those small charges seemed excessive to me. I couldn't see the justification for them.

Now I understand why I was so irate; God enabled me to understand that what I envisioned then is what we are experiencing now. A few years ago, could you have envisioned that you would be charged one dollar each time you made a deposit or withdrawal without using your bank-printed deposit or withdrawal slips?

Get Out Your Calculator!

If you would take the time to add up your monthly bank fees, then multiply them by twelve months, you would probably discover a nice little tin can savings deposit that could have been yours. Imagine...a one-dollar charge for not using a printed deposit or withdrawal slip! You should not continue to ignore this senselessness. This substantiates what I have been saying about newfound, creative fees. And I believe they're going to get even more creative as time goes on and banks continue to merge. Someone has to pay the bill—why not us?

Think About It—
The banking community has been winning a psychological game of finance with us by hypnotizing us into believing their charges have been for our best.

Banking institutions have always made huge sums of

money by lending your deposits at top interest—including lending it back to you. But that wasn't enough. Your deposits in their institutions became too appealing to just "sit" there and accumulate at the interest rate they agreed to pay you for allowing them to loan and invest it. So they figured an ingenious way of snatching back that little interest they paid you—through fees.

Excessive fees and usury can throw one literally into bankruptcy. No wonder bankruptcies are continuously on the rise. Today's high fees and charges can exhaust families' funds, causing horrendous financial setbacks and problems. At the rate they have been increasing, I believe the amount of new fees and charges on the horizon may soon exceed many take-home wages. **Fees are increasing more rapidly than today's hourly wages. It will take a sweeping change of events—and even a miracle—to beat this hungry system, because you can't feed greed. After you've given all you've got, it's still not enough. Greed's appetite is insatiable!** Your deposits are swallowed by a blood-thirsty, vampire banking system that wants your blood. Its goal is to drain you to death financially.

So I say to you again—put your trust in God's financial institution. There, your deposits never have a fee applied to them. And God's interest rate is phenomenal, boasting thirtyfold, sixtyfold, and one hundredfold plus returns. Not only that, but in God's financial system:

1. There are no late charges or penalties for withdrawals.
2. There are certainly no charges for deposits.
3. There are no teller fees.
4. There are no ATM charges.
5. **As an added bonus, there are no thieves who have access or can get in—including bankers.**

Building Wealth Using the Tin Can Method

I personally define a *fee* as *free* money...a "trumped-up charge" legalized by the system. It's legalized cheating, okay? Maybe that term is more understandable. It is a charge that, if allowed, will appear again tomorrow at a slightly higher rate or under the guise of a new, more creative and innovative program. Soon, someone may approach you on the street and say, "You owe me a fee."

"What for?" you will ask.

"For walking past me," they will reply. Or, "For breathing, or just being alive."

The dead are the only ones who are "fee-free." They can't be charged anymore. They have already been "fee'd" to death.

So choose God. Stay fee free as you get free.

NSF—Non Sense Fee

> And they are as greedy as dogs never satisfied. They are stupid shepherds, all following their own, all of them intent on personal gain.
> —Isaiah 56:11, NLT

The world's system won't get any better—it will only worsen. If we the people continue to allow these strongmen to get their hands in our pockets, we may never be able to get their hands out. They are constantly looking for more and more creative ways to charge us fees, legally or illegally. Even if it proves to be illegal, by the time all the rhetoric and court processes run their course, a year or two has passed while millions are made by these legalized crooks. Lots of businesses are allowed to charge us fees due to politics—"You wash my hands, and I'll wash yours."

The Business Side of Hell

We've discussed the depositor side of the escalating NSF

charges, which are charging bank customers thirty dollars or more for insufficient checks. Now I want to talk a little more about the business side of that fee. Pay careful attention to this ridiculous and unjustifiable fee. A customer walks in and makes a purchase from your company, perhaps two hundred dollars. But the check returned to you is stamped NSF. You as the business owner are charged a fee of four dollars or more by your bank for the customer that wrote the check.

Now, of course you should have known that the check was going to be returned, because, after all, you have *clairvoyant abilities,* right? How could any business know in advance that the check it's receiving from a customer is going to be returned? If the business establishment knew this, do you think they would accept the check in the first place? So ethically, the blame, and cost if there has to be one, should be placed upon the customer, not on the business.

Meanwhile, the bank where the check was drawn charges that customer an enormous fee, thirty dollars or more. The bad check could have been an honest mistake. The customer could be a long-standing, honest patron who mistakenly forgot to deduct a new draft. Or his direct deposit may not have been received and posted in time because the bank's computers were down. Possibly his spouse forgot to make the deposit on time or the bank itself made an ugly error.

No matter. The fee charger's hands have already found their way in your pockets—and out again. The bank is quite happy about it. And even if they happen to discover that the reason for the NSF fee proves to be their own fault, the four dollars charged to the business has been deducted— never to be seen again. You'll never be reimbursed for it. Bam! What a scam! Your four dollars are gone just like that! You see the charge and say, "Well, at least it wasn't four hundred dollars, or even forty dollars." But when you add your four dollar fee (legally or illegally deducted) to the thousands of other businesses who have no idea their customers' checks are going to bounce, they add up to millions. And that's a hefty financial eye-opener!

> **THINK ABOUT IT—**
> *THEY TELL US TO PUT OUR MONEY INTO BANKS BECAUSE IT IS SAFER, BUT HOW SAFE CAN IT BE WHEN THE BANKS ARE TAKING IT OUT AS FAST AS WE PUT IT IN?*

We are being charged for being imperfect human beings—just as they were imperfect human beings when we bailed them out of their savings and loan crisis. But when their customers make a mistake, or you as the business owner are passed a bad check, there is no bail out, there is no forgiveness coming from them. According to them, all transactions are accurate at banks, because their *robot machines* are perfect. Right?

INVOLUNTARY AUTOMATIC DEPOSIT

They have even stooped to the point of enticing the company you work for to put your entire paycheck into their possession through the use of direct deposit—whether you like it or not. I suppose you aren't smart enough to deposit your own check. I suppose they figure they are doing you, the American public, a favor! The sad part about this is that you, or someone else, is bound to get fee'd in the process.

I don't know about you, but I'm an adult, and I want to be respected and treated as such. Therefore, when I get paid, I want to hold my check in my hand before my eyes, not some pay stub. I labored for the money, so why should the bank, who labored not, receive the privilege of seeing my paycheck or stub *first?* I believe the banks know that if more people understood these issues, many wouldn't deposit their checks in their banks or even open checking accounts, thus denying the banks more fee profits.

Sound farfetched? No, none of this is crazy or farfetched thinking. Had you foreseen a time when you would be paying a fee to use a human teller? Did you ever think you would be paying a fee to deposit or take your money out of a bank? Did you foresee many of the fees that are being charged today, with new ones coming up in so many areas? NO! Of course you didn't. No one did.

There are many culprits that rob us of potential savings. Some are of our own misdoing, others are the doing of the system. We need to recognize each one in order to loosen its grasp on our pockets. God's Financial Academy of Accountability is where the buck should start and stop.

THE WORD OF GOD SPEAKS INTO EVERY SITUATION

Much of God's written Word deals with social and political issues. The Bible speaks out against injustice in every form. It speaks truth in the midst of a lie. God desires His people to prosper. He truly wants us to live and eat the good of the land. He wants us to lend (without charging usury) so we don't have to borrow, but not at the expense of oppressing others.

God has never been against man having things—*He's against things having man*. When that happens, man becomes selfish, greedy, and self-destructive.

God's written Word reveals the reasons we exist under a curse. It is up to us to turn the tables on the godless practices of our day.

Many of the problems we encounter are own faults, but some of them come from man's system. We have been disobedient children, so God's mercy and grace is calling us one more time to get it right. This simple tin can savings message is bigger and more powerful and diverse than even

Building Wealth Using the Tin Can Method

I can conceive, just as I'm sure Moses had no earthly idea that God would use his simple rod to produce such awesome miracles. Oh, what our God can do with simple things!

So don't take this tin can message lightly. God made the rod, and He fashioned the tin. Both are products of His doing. The last chapter of Revelation tells us to let the unjust be unjust still, and let the righteous be righteous still (Rev. 22:11). God is saying, "My people (individually and collectively as a nation), get in order. Be obedient. I'm a merciful and gracious God. Don't put other gods before Me. I'm a jealous God, a terrible God. Do not tempt Me!"

To our current government, He is saying, "You have made it hard for My people to serve and obey Me. You have robbed Me. Because it has been easy for you to rob Me, you are robbing My people. Your heart is hard. You have heaped your treasures and riches—but the miseries to come will cause you to howl and weep. Repent I say! Repent!"

Think About It—
Remember, those who insist on having it all . . . usually wind up with nothing.

When will the fee craze stop? Never! That is, unless we the people demand otherwise. I say this prophetically. Watch and see! **Many institutions have found the fee and tax gold vein.** Many roundtable discussions have taken place while you have been reading this book to invent new *ghost services* and *charges* to justify new fees and make more money. Let's look at a few of the fees these discussions have produced so far:

A List of Offensive Fees and Taxes (not exhaustive)

- *New car sales tax*—add to that the licensing fee tax every year that the car is owned. If car is purchased via

FEES FROM HELL

financing, interest is not allowed as a tax deduction.
- *General "stuff" tax*—in some states every possession owned is taxed annually, even though sales taxes were paid at the time of purchase.
- *New appliance tax*—paid when purchased.
- *Credit cards fees*—charges of 18 to 25 percent for using OPM. Many give 4 percent or less fees for using your money.
- *IRS fees*—the more you give them, the more they mess up.
- *City and county taxes*—residents pay both in some states.
- *Increased cable fees.*
- *Used vehicle purchase fee*—the purpose given for this new gouge is said to be to get rid of old vehicles. If that's true, why is the one wanting to get rid of the vehicle charged a fee?
- *Dry cleaning fee tax.*
- *Hotel taxes* (occupancy and etc.)
- *New and exciting sanitation taxes*—fees for collection of waste or fees when you fail to remove your container from the road. Someone has calculated how to increase their profits through your forgetfulness!
- *Department store card fees for nonusage.*
- *Nonusage of certain phone company long distance calls.*
- *Touchtone telephone fee*—a fee for touching the phone? How can you use it without touching it?
- *First time doctor's office visit fee*—chart, office call, etc.
- *Credit check fee.*
- *Incorrect deposit slip information fee* normally $5 (human error fee for recording incorrect amount).
- *Inventory tax*—charged retailers annually for unsold items.
- *Inheritances taxes*—the Word says a good man will leave an inheritance to his children's children. This is

Building Wealth Using the Tin Can Method

made difficult by a system that snatches a large portion of what one has labored to leave to family. Inheritance has been taxed already, so this is a tax upon a tax.
- *Food tax*—every one has to eat, rich and poor alike.
- *Airline ticket tax.*
- *Car rental tax.*

This is a very limited list. But we should at least learn something from their greedy methods. Their fees are usually never enough to make anyone irate, but they add and add and add up! Fifty cents, one dollar, two dollars or more **collected or saved** can equal thousands and even millions of dollars. And the tin can method can work for *you,* not *them.*

Think About It—
The world's business system doesn't despise five or ten cents. Why should you?

If you want to challenge this statement, ask any of today's long distance telephone companies, such as AT&T, SPRINT, or MCI. They all want your business for ten cents a minute or more—ten cents a minute times millions of people calling will eventually equal millions. But we are so complacent that we seldom take the time to analyze the fees these various businesses and institutions have exacted upon us. **We simply haven't realized the importance and power of the "small change" they're collecting.**

Speak Up—Speak Out!

I believe the reason many people don't have a savings of any kind is because of these various fees from hell. So speak up! Every day we give a small fortune away in cents and dollars to anyone who taxes or fees us unfairly—and we say nothing about it because it is such a seemingly small amount. There is no outrage.

But it is time to speak up and stop giving away our cents and dollars. It's time to stop respecting those entities who have been charging us more than we respect ourselves by holding them accountable. It is time to start asking them whether these fees are fair, legal, or illegal. If you don't speak up, who will? We the people have the power to stop a lot of this nonsense that has been affecting us physically and financially. But we must speak up! It is time to stop making our small change mole hills into mountains by passing it off as insignificant chunk change. America's government, banking, and business establishments know and understand it. And now, so do you.

I believe the tax and fee increases we are seeing today will be one of the key instruments the master manipulator, the devourer, will use to deceive the world into worldwide poverty, lack, and debt. All this money funneling into the wrong hands will only cause an evil dominant rule over good, and sincere people who aren't wise enough to know they are being woven into a web of financial disaster.

We the people have been naive for too long. We must take control to stop the powers that be from getting anymore out of control. A greedy man's insatiable appetite can never be completely fulfilled or satisfied. We must rise up and nip this thing in the bud. If we don't, these fees, taxes, and small new corporate charges will continue to rise to astronomical levels.

Become a better watchman over what is yours, and know all of the in's and out's of Satan's operations. You are the one who works and earns your pennies and dollars. **Just watch their reaction when you start holding them accountable.** Then it will become significant. If it can make them rich, just think about the small fortune you could amass to make you rich plus spread the gospel—the power of God is in your corner. But we are more disciplined in paying others than ourselves. Strange, isn't it? Many are more prone to give into someone else's tin can instead of their own. Then they prosper—and you don't.

INVOLUNTARY "SAVE MOTHER EARTH" FEE

A couple of years ago the city in which I live delivered to every resident a bright red plastic bin about the size of a regular clothes basket. It had something to do with the helping of the environment through recycling. The residents were to put plastic bottles into this red bin. It didn't seem to matter whether we wanted to participate in this recycling project or not—I don't think we were given a choice. Each resident received one of these bright red bins. Shortly thereafter, each household received a little addition to their monthly utility bill in the form of a two dollar fee.

Now I haven't once used this red plastic bin since it was delivered to my door step. You would figure that two dollars a month times one year would pay for this cheap thing in full, making any other monthly additions to that bill unnecessary. But this kind of thinking doesn't take into account the insatiable appetite of greed, because the next year the monthly fee jumped from two dollars to three dollars. Now it is nearly five dollars.

Mind you, I know some city residents are using these bins, so you would think that some of these containers would be a little used or worn by now. But to my knowledge, none of the bins have been replaced. I predict the cost will continue to rise in the form of increased fees for these cheap baskets, and that they will continue to increase as long as the city can get away with it.

WAKE UP!

The homeowners are the ones who should be paid or given

a credit toward their bill. Why? They do the work of **sorting**—not the city—by putting the plastic containers in these things. This is just another example of free-money fees that are creeping in among us. The evil nature of greed is never satisfied with mere cents and dollars. If you don't put your foot down now, one day your pay check won't be sufficient to cover all fees and compounding small charges.

Think about taxes. With each new tax increase since the end of World War II, we have paid them. Today, after paying every tax and fee connected with our purchases and regular income, 50 percent flows into the government's coffers. This is our money, which is wasted due to their reckless spending habits—just like they didn't ask for our permission when they took our money to bail out the bankers in the savings and loan scandals. What will you use when the combination of these fees is so expensive that you can't pay your regular bills along with them?

An Example From Nehemiah

But be of good courage, because there is still time to make your voice known. There is still time to rebuild the walls of your own finances, just as Nehemiah was called to do in rebuilding Jerusalem. When we return to God, He will return to us, as it is written in Nehemiah 1:9:

> But if ye turn unto me, and keep my commandments, and do them; though there were of you cast out unto the uttermost part of the heaven, yet will I gather them from thence, and will bring them unto the place that I have chosen to set my name there.
> —Nehemiah 1:9

We need the mercy of God for this day and the days to come. It will be those of us who desire to fear and obey His name who will prosper. Let Nehemiah serve as a good

Building Wealth Using the Tin Can Method

example. In Nehemiah 2 the people of God had been scattered, and their land had been left wasted and desolate. The walls of Jerusalem had been broken, and the gates had been burned. Nehemiah had great remorse in his heart for Jerusalem and God's people, so he wept and prayed earnestly to God for Jerusalem.

God gave Nehemiah great favor with the Persian King Artaxerxes, who allowed Nehemiah to fulfill his desire of rebuilding Jerusalem's walls. But there were evil men that laughed at Nehemiah's righteous plans, just as Satan will cause people to laugh and put some type of stumbling block in your path to hinder or disgust you in spirit. Nehemiah and his company were scorned, but they knew the order of God's mission. We need to follow Nehemiah's response and stamina as our example:

> The God of Heaven, He will prosper us, therefore we His servants will arise and build, but you [Satan] have no portion nor right, nor memorial in Jerusalem.
> —NEHEMIAH 20:20

I like that response! When the world laughs at us, let's follow Nehemiah's simple and direct-to-the-point example. When God is for you, who can be against you?

Exalt the Word of God when you start your small savings as the enemy laughs and says, "You're crazy to try to save. Besides, what's the big deal with these little fees? The bankers have a right to charge for their services! Starting with a dollar, you will never get ahead!" When you hear this, remember Nehemiah's words: "The God of Heaven, He will prosper me"—*regardless!*

Remember this: Nehemiah sought to rebuild the desolate walls of Jerusalem without the needed money or naturally required materials to accomplish his task. He had nothing but his trust in God. And why not? He's a big God. He owns the cattle on a thousand hills. The earth is His and the fullness thereof and all that dwell therein! God didn't ask Nehemiah how much equipment or money he had to embark upon the task. It really didn't matter. What did matter was that Nehemiah was willing to depend upon God and do what was right with what he had. Then he moved and trusted God to supply all he would need. And God gave him favor whenever it was needed.

Remember that a little bit of anything with a whole lot of favor will go many times further than what you do or don't have in your hands. As you exemplify godly obedience, God will bring the increase. If God can rebuild a temple from ruins, certainly He can rebuild your finances. Just give Him something to work with along with your obedience.

Satan wants you to *stop* or to *not start* at all. He tries to hinder you through his many fees—fees from hell. The devourer wants to tax and fee you into poverty. Legal or illegal, it makes no difference to him. The devil knows that when God's people stand up and say, "Enough is enough!" it will affect his evil kingdom, because right now most of the world's wealth lies in the hands of Satan's servants.

A Banker Lesson

The small beginnings of the tin can method are not to be despised. The process of starting with little to grow into much is God's idea. The banking systems I have criticized certainly know this. We should be smart enough to take a lesson from them.

Everyone who has an account of some kind with any bank pays some type of service fee. They know the two dollars a month or more we blow off as insignificant times 1 million people equals 2 million dollars plus. So why can't you do the same for yourself? Pay yourself week by week, month by month, year by year. It adds up on a consistent basis. Pennies, nickels, and dimes will grow into multiplied thousands as we entrust them to God's righteous care.

BUILDING WEALTH USING THE TIN CAN METHOD

By now I hope that you now believe two dollars—more or less—is worth saving. And I hope you have been putting your money daily into your own tin can. We can no longer afford to sit by idly doing nothing. Let's bring Satan's kingdom down *now*. He's been ruling long enough. The banks have no money unless we deposit ours. Read the fine print from now on. Then hold them accountable and shop for a better deal. If enough of us do it, they'll get the picture. Write your state and federal government, including God's Word. Let them know that enough is enough!

But most importantly, let God through your obedience reverse the curse off your finances and prosper you above the world's "hook-and-crook" measures. Give God His tithes and offerings. Then trust and watch His supernatural multiplication table begin to work for you as the wealth of the wicked takes wings and flies away.

Ten
Excusers, Abusers, and Misusers

Many people are adept at explaining away their responsibility for what goes wrong in their lives, including not saving. Instead of candidly admitting, "I'm wrong; I was wasteful; I was selfish"; or "I acted foolishly with my money," they use other excuses. I call them excusers, abusers, and misusers. If this is you, it's time to change. It is vital that you pray for our nation and speak out on the injustices of usury and fees, because man will get away with what he can until he is caught and held to account. But it is even more important that you begin mending your own financial ways if your ways have not been the ways of God as revealed in His Word. His ways consist of tithing, believing, giving offerings, and saving. So let's talk again about saving.

The poor, middle class, and upper-class rich all participate in some form of unfruitful wastefulness. No one—and I mean no one—is exempt. Most classes are robbing God. It doesn't matter whether you keep a record or not, because God does. He has never ever miscalculated, and He never will! The charts in this chapter consist of various unproductive habits that can be eliminated or curtailed, depending upon which of them may be hindering the beginning of a savings plan for you. By eliminating or cutting back on one

Building Wealth Using the Tin Can Method

or more of these indulgences, you will be given a new source of funds to increase your tin can. Sometimes a simple chart can put things into an instantly clear perspective and wake us up into reality. Some of you have no idea how much you are spending on your habits; these visual aids will make it clear. A picture can truly be worth a thousand of words.

Face it! Your financial mess needs a doctor. Quick! You need a specialist in the field of finances. You don't need "Doctor Feel Good" (a raise). You need "Doctor True Heart" (obedience and discipline). Yes, someone who will get to the truth of your financial problems, diagnose, expose, and if allowed, guide you toward the proper treatment. Your appointment has been set for today. The Great Financial Physician is ready to see you immediately, and this is what He says:

Are You Savings Poor?

Cause: You are out of order and disobedient. You show poor stewardship over what God has entrusted into your hands.
Prognosis: You are savings poor.
Recommended Treatment: Pay tithes and offerings (your foundation). Get in order. Start saving or building your wealth using the tin can.

Stop despising small beginnings (a mindset principle).

DO YOU DO THE FOLLOWING? (CIRCLE ONE)

Do you spend money for lottery tickets?	YES	NO
Do you buy lunch every day?	YES	NO
Do you play Bingo?	YES	NO
Do you daily take your children out to eat at fast-food restaurants?	YES	NO
Do you buy cigarettes every day?	YES	NO
Do you buy beer every day?	YES	NO
Do you buy a new car every year?	YES	NO

Excusers, Abusers, and Misusers

Do you buy only name-brand sneakers for your children?
   (Do not allow your children to be sneaker rich
      and savings poor.)   YES   NO
Do you buy cars you can't afford?   YES   NO
Do you spoil your children by buying
   them only famous, designer clothes?   YES   NO
Do you spend money for illegal drugs?   YES   NO
Do you rent videos each week on a consistent basis?   YES   NO

VIDEO RENTALS

(Amounts referenced below are based on three movie rentals twice a week at a cost of $3.50 per movie.)

WEEK	WEEKLY SUBTOTAL	TOTAL
WEEK #1	$21.00	$21.00
WEEK #2	$21.00	$42.00
WEEK #3	$21.00	$63.00
WEEK #4	$21.00	$84.00
	Monthly Total	$84.00
	Yearly Total	$1,008.00

If you carefully observe the above, you will note that one month of renting videos will cost you $84.00. One year of renting videos at $84.00 per month for twelve months equals $1,008.00.
Do you have $1,008.00 in a savings account?

BINGO/GAMBLING

Learn to save the money you've been trying to win.

> Ill-gotten gain has no lasting value, but right living can save your life.
>   —PROVERBS 10:2, NLT

Building Wealth Using the Tin Can Method

> Wealth gotten by vanity shall be diminished; but he that gathereth by labour shall increase.
> —Proverbs 13:11

Gambling has brought many "big wigs" down, stripping them and their families of their fortunes. It has even caused many to take their own lives due to indebtedness. For the gambler, hundreds in hand today can easily become millions in debt tomorrow. It's just a matter of turning up the wrong card, spinning the wrong number, flipping losing dice, or betting the wrong hand. It takes only minutes. Fortunes that took years to amass can be lost in a moment! Whether for big stakes or little stakes, in the end you always lose. From jacks to Bingo, it devours your finances like a piranha devours flesh. It is more absorbent than a sponge. It's more deadly than a viper. Yet many Americans live to gamble and gamble to live. Even our government has made "evil" legal.

I can recall years ago, when the innocent game of Bingo was just a fun pastime game to idle one's time away. It was clean and somewhat wholesome. Just being able to say "bingo" before anyone else was sufficient enough of a thrill for the winner. But today it has been carried to a new level and ranks with big-time gambling. I was naively shocked to learn what the game today has become in terms of cost. The stakes can be plenty big. So big, in fact, that its losers can become "bingo poor."

As I began to do some real investigating on this subject, I asked myself, "Just where do these all-the-time-grumbling, I-don't-get-paid-enough, I'm-broke, I-need-help people get these resources to play?"

I can see how those who are business owners or high-salaried corporate Americans may be able to come up with the money. But everyday, ordinary, salaried three-kids-at-home, two-kids-in-college, two-bedroom-home, two-car-payment-paying, no-savings-account-people who play the game I just can't seem to understand. The truth of the matter is that many people would give their *last* dime toward a *chance*. It amazes me how one can so eagerly pay fifty cents or more a game toward a chance while at the same time think it's absurd to pay that same fifty cents into a daily savings program. The fifty cents put into your tin can will be there tomorrow; the other gambled in hopes of winning a bingo pot will never be seen again.

I was talking with a hairdresser I hired to do my daughter's hair not long ago, and after her husband dropped her off, she said, "I have about another hour or so to go before I'm done. If my husband calls, tell him I'll be finished around that time, then he can come and pick me up. This is good timing," she said. "The place where he will be coming from is a bingo house, and this is about the time it closes."

"A bingo house?" I asked.

"Yes," she responded. "He loves to play Bingo. That's his fun."

"How often does he play?" I asked.

"Almost every night," she replied.

"Really? Does he win?" I asked.

"Sometimes he does. But more often than not, he doesn't win anything. Still, he loves it. He has to do something. You see, he once drank heavily, until he developed a health problem from smoking, and his doctor told him to stop. So he took up Bingo to fill the void." I quickly found out that this man left one addiction to save his health only to embark on another that affected his wealth.

As I began very tenderly, without becoming too inquisitive, asking to see how this woman felt about her husband's newfound addiction, she told me she wasn't overjoyed about it. But she was happy that it wouldn't kill him, like smoking. Then she dropped the bomb shell on me when I learned how much he invested in this game. The last time I played Bingo, it was almost free and just for fun. I knew

Building Wealth Using the Tin Can Method

some games had gone up to fifty cents or a dollar. But I was knocked off my feet when she told me he spent $25 to $30 a night. "What?" I responded. "You've got to be kidding!"

"No I'm not," she stated. "My husband plays maybe three, four, or five times a week, and he loses anywhere between $25 to $30 a night—that is unless he wins the pot—which isn't that often."

She must mean $25 to $30 a week, surely not that much per night, I thought to myself initially. Needless, to say, she wasn't mistaken, and my mental calculator went to work. This is what I found:

*NOTE: As is with all scales throughout this book, the amount could be substantially higher or lower for another person. This man was a "low roller" compared to others who spend much more.

Bingo-Playing Finances

Many play on Sunday night as well, however it's shocking enough for the days of the week, so I omitted Sunday (worship day).

- represents losing
+ represents winning

WEEK #1

Monday night Bingo	-25.00
Tuesday night Bingo	-25.00
Wednesday night Bingo	-25.00
Thursday night Bingo	-25.00
Friday night Bingo	-25.00
Saturday night Bingo	-20.00
TOTAL WEEK #1	**-145.00**

WEEK #2

Monday night Bingo	-25.00
Tuesday night Bingo	-25.00
Wednesday night Bingo	-25.00
Thursday night Bingo	-25.00
Friday night Bingo	-20.00
Saturday night Bingo	-20.00
TOTAL WEEK #2	**-140.00**

WEEK #3

Monday night Bingo	-20.00
Tuesday night Bingo	-20.00
Wednesday night Bingo	-20.00
Thursday night Bingo	-20.00
Friday night Bingo	-25.00
Saturday night Bingo	-20.00
TOTAL WEEK #3	**-125.00**

So far, if you've been counting (and the whole point of this is to make sure you start), this man spent $410.00 in three weeks "just for fun." Now put on your thinking cap: This is equivalent to a house payment, a car note, or weekend trip. It would certainly add up to a wonderful tin can amount after giving God that which belongs to Him. But the truth of the matter is, this kind of money is being devoured by Satan every day around the world, and it is a stench in the nostrils of God. How many souls do you think could have been saved . . . how many hungry fed with these kinds of resources applied to God's work?

So you say you don't make enough to tithe? And you say you can't save anything? *But you do make enough to gamble for fun?* I tell you, God will not continue to stand by and allow this to go on. My dear brothers and sisters in Christ, either we *shape up* or get *shipped out*. Choose this day

Building Wealth Using the Tin Can Method

whom you will serve. God is a jealous God, and He won't have any other gods (games included) before Him. Either you will respect and obey Him, or respect, obey, and honor man. You can't serve two gods. The Word says either you will love one or you will hate the other. You cannot serve God and mammon (Luke 16:13).

Let's continue with the chart:

WEEK #4

Monday night Bingo	
(They won the $100.00 jackpot)	+100.00
Tuesday night Bingo	-20.00
Wednesday night Bingo	-20.00
Thursday night Bingo	-25.00
Friday night Bingo	-25.00
Saturday night Bingo	
(They won the $100 jackpot)	+100.00
TOTAL WEEK #4	**+110.00**

Now the winning has enticed and entrapped him even more to continue.

WEEK #5

Monday night Bingo	-25.00
Tuesday night Bingo	-25.00
Wednesday night Bingo	-25.00
Thursday night Bingo	-25.00
Friday night Bingo	-25.00
Saturday night Bingo	
(Did not play—low on cash)	0.00
TOTAL WEEK #5	**-125.00**

He lost his $110.00 plus another $15.00 in Week #5, and he was right back where he started.

WEEK #6

Monday night Bingo	-25.00
Tuesday night Bingo	-25.00
Wednesday night Bingo	-25.00
Thursday night Bingo	-25.00
Friday night Bingo	-25.00
Saturday night Bingo	
(Did not play—low on cash)	0.00
TOTAL WEEK #6	**-125.00**

By the end of week #6, our player has a serious shortage of cash. Let's see how that could affect his future finances.

A new, upcoming, rising stock was offered to the workers in his company on Monday morning of week seven. The shares were five cents in increments of five hundred. The expected rise of shares in six months would be three dollars. This offer would not be repeated again, and any takers had to act within twenty-four hours.

Our player couldn't take advantage of offer because he couldn't afford to.

The five hundred shares at five cents per share would have cost our player $25. One night of not playing Bingo and putting the $25 into a tin can would have amassed him the $25 needed. The rising of the shares at the expected three dollars per share in the six months predicted would have netted him $1,500. So, this good deal brought about by God was unable to be taken advantage of because he was an out-of-order, undisciplined, bingo-poor steward of what God had blessed him with.

"Many," the Lord is saying, "of these kinds of deals I am able to bring or put before My people. But they are not ready. I will only hold back for so long. Those who have ears to hear, hear, and eyes to see, see. Those who are obedient will receive a pouring upon of bountiful good deals. I will not continue to wait on the disobedient. My people must get in order. I will not continue to hold back. Will you be ready? Will you get ready?"

Now, if you want to know something that is really funny and ironic—if you were to ask these same bingo players if they could afford to save $125 a week out of their salaries, they would look at you as if you were an alien from Pluto. They would say, "Who can save that kind of money a week? I don't make that kind of salary. Yes, I would like to, but I certainly can't afford to. That's a lot of money to save out of one's salary a week. No! I can't afford to, but it would be nice." And all the while, they are so blinded by their foolishness that they can't even see they had it all along. **Gambling** has entangled and blinded them. They never stop to tally how much they spend per night. They just do it! It's regarded as normal as hygienic daily care.

Let's total that six weeks of Bingo-ing:

WINS OR LOSSES	
Bingo Week #1	-145.00
Bingo Week #2	-140.00
Bingo Week #3	-125.00
Bingo Week #4	+110.00
Bingo Week #5	-125.00
Bingo Week #6	-125.00
Total spent in six weeks	**-$550.00**

THINK ABOUT IT—
THIS PLAYER IS CONSIDERED BY BIG-TIME MONEY PLAYERS AS A LITTLE FISH. NEVERTHELESS, THE LOSS OF $550.00 IN SIX WEEKS IS A TRAGEDY.

There Is No Shortage of Money

I recall not too long ago that a singer had been commissioned by a rich oil sultan to perform before five hundred people in a private show for the sultan's niece's birthday. The singer and her entourage had to sign confidentiality forms stating they would say nothing about what they saw. When an interviewer asked one of them what the sultan's 1,800-plus room castle was like, that person's response was, "All I know is that it was beyond belief. Everything was gold. Gold doors, gold this, gold that. . . ."

Listen, people, there is no shortage of money. Even though this man may be regarded as the richest man in the world, his "lot" is still a "little" compared to what is *untouched and untapped*. It is waiting for us, God's people, to get in line and in order so He can open and reveal His treasures to His children.

I personally believe that we, God's people, are holding up the revealing of God's blessings. Satan, the god of gambling, has deceived and robbed many. Bingo player (and gamblers), how long will you be bewitched? I pray the following charts—combined with the power of the Holy Spirit—will shake you into reality. Stop misusing what God has blessed and entrusted to you.

"And I will give you treasures hidden in the darkness—secret riches. I will do this so you may know that I am the Lord" (Isa. 45:3, NLT). But to splurge what we presently have upon gambling will forfeit it from our grasp.

Don't Gamble Rich and Become Savings Poor

Now I want to show you what a year of Bingo would cost. And just for fun, I want you to compare your savings account statement to see if you can get a match. We will use the one-and-a-half-month scale from our previous figures, equaling $550.00 for each six-week period.

Building Wealth Using the Tin Can Method

A Year of Bingo	
1. 1st 6 Weeks	-550.00
2. 2nd 6 Weeks	-550.00
3. 3rd 6 Weeks	-550.00
4. 4th 6 Weeks	-550.00
5. 5th 6 Weeks	-550.00
6. 6th 6 Weeks	-550.00
7. 7th 6 Weeks	-550.00
8. 8th 6 Weeks	-550.00
9. Remaining four-week period	-300.00
Twelve-month total (52 weeks) equals a loss of $4,700.00.	

Can you match this? Your savings versus your loss? Have you put $4,700 into a savings account over the past year? Do you think you make enough money to give tithes and offerings and save? I should say so, if this scale fits you.

This must stop! Proverbs 8:21 says, "Those who love me [obedient] inherit wealth, for I fill their treasures"(NLT). God has not blessed you nor given you the power to get wealth to squander it away on Bingo gambling when there are many who are lost and hurting who need salvation. The money is there, but the gospel hasn't reached them because of your squandering. If you can pay to play Bingo, you can pay your tithes and offerings and yes, even save (tin can) or pay yourself. And I believe this money will cease to be available for those who continue in such foolishness.

From the poor to the rich, gambling accepts any one foolish enough to play. It doesn't discriminate. Only one criterion is needed—**your hard-earned money.**

Many Christians and non-Christians indulge in this most popular and addictive pastime under the guise of sport or game. Some play seriously, and some play "just for fun." But either way, those who engage in it may as well flush their hard-earned money down the toilet. Because gambling

Excusers, Abusers, and Misusers

is set up to lose. And *losing money is neither funny or fun.*

Satan has such a way of distorting things. He's just what the Word says he is, a liar from the pit of hell. He will cause you to believe that "right is wrong" and "wrong is right." He clinches your mentality and grips your better judgment. Bingo is no longer Bingo; it is a high-stakes scam.

Now let's look at a chart showing possible losses in what is the biggest gambling operation ever perpetrated on America—the lottery.

Think About It—

IF YOU HAD IN YOUR TIN CAN ALL THE MONEY YOU'VE SPENT IN PLAYING THE LOTTERY DAILY, WEEKLY, MONTHLY, OR YEARLY, HOW MUCH WOULD YOU BE WORTH TODAY?

$3 LOTTERY (NUMBER) PLAYERS
(Based on spending $3 per day, excluding Saturday and Sunday.)

WEEK	WEEKLY SUBTOTAL	TOTAL
WEEK #1	Monday –$3.00	
	Tuesday–$3.00	
	Wednesday–$3.00	
	Thursday–$3.00	
	Friday–$3.00	
	Weekly Total–$15.00	$15.00
WEEK #2	$15.00	$30.00
WEEK #3	$15.00	$45.00
WEEK #4	$15.00	$60.00

One month of playing the lottery at $3 per day equals $60.00.
One year of playing the lottery at $3 per day equals $720.00.
Five years of playing the lottery at $3 per day equals $3,600.
DO YOU HAVE $3,600 IN A SAVINGS ACCOUNT?

$5 LOTTERY (NUMBER) PLAYERS
(Based on spending $5 per day, excluding Sunday.)

WEEK	WEEKLY SUBTOTAL		TOTAL
WEEK #1	Monday–$5.00		
	Tuesday–$5.00		
	Wednesday–$5.00		
	Thursday–$5.00		
	Friday–$5.00		
	Saturday$5.00		
	Weekly Total	$30.00	$30.00
WEEK #2		$30.00	$60.00
WEEK #3		$30.00	$90.00
WEEK #4		$30.00	$120.00

THINK ABOUT IT—
YOU DON'T WANT TO GIVE GOD ONE DOLLAR ON SUNDAY, YET YOU SPEND FIVE DOLLARS (OR EVEN $50!) A DAY ON THE LOTTERY. WITH THIS KIND OF MONEY, THE GOSPEL COULD BE PREACHED TO ALL THE NATIONS. IT'S NOT THE PREACHERS WHO ARE AFTER YOUR MONEY—YOU'RE THROWING IT AWAY, AND NO ONE (AND NO MONEY) IS BEING SAVED.

One month of playing the lottery at $5 per day equals $120.00.
One year of playing the lottery at $5 per day equals $1,440.00.
Five years of playing the lottery at $5 per day equals $7,200.00.
DO YOU HAVE $7,200 IN A SAVINGS ACCOUNT?
NOTE: This player is asking to borrow money daily for lunch!

$10 LOTTERY(NUMBER) PLAYERS
(Based on spending $10 per day, excluding Saturday and Sunday.)

WEEK	WEEKLY SUBTOTAL	TOTAL
WEEK #1	Monday–$10.00	
	Tuesday–$10.00	
	Wednesday–$10.00	
	Thursday–$10.00	
	Friday–$10.00	
	Weekly Total $50.00	$50.00
WEEK #2	$50.00	$100.00
WEEK #3	$50.00	$150.00
WEEK #4	$50.00	$200.00

One month of playing the lottery at $10 per day equals $200.00.
One year of playing the lottery at $10 per day equals $2,400.
Five years of playing the lottery at $10 per day equals $12,000.
DO YOU HAVE $12,000.IN A SAVINGS ACCOUNT? NO! THE LOTTERY HAS IT.

$50 LOTTERY(NUMBER) PLAYERS
(Based on spending $50 per day, excluding Saturday and Sunday.)

WEEK	WEEKLY SUBTOTAL	TOTAL
WEEK #1	Monday–$50.00	
	Tuesday–$50.00	
	Wednesday–$50.00	
	Thursday–$50.00	
	Friday–$50.00	
	Weekly Total $250.00	$250.00
WEEK #2	$250.00	$500.00
WEEK #3	$250.00	$750.00
WEEK #4	$250.00	$1,000.00

Building Wealth Using the Tin Can Method

One month of playing the lottery at $50 per day equals $1,000.
One year of playing the lottery at $50 per day equals $12,000.
Five years of playing the lottery at $50 per day equals $60,000.
DO YOU HAVE $60,000 IN A SAVINGS ACCOUNT?
NOTE: Only a fool would throw away this kind of money. Yes, I called you a *fool,* and the Word supports it. (See Proverbs 21:20.)

Social Drinkers—Money Shrinkers

There are many different patterns of alcohol abuse. A variety of social, financial, and medical problems result from high-risk drinking. Statistics show that social drinking produces abuse just as chronic addiction produces abuse. There is a severity involved in mixing alcohol and work. Businesses want a drug-free workplace that is conducive for them to receive the optimum work performance from their employees. It is said that where you find drugs at work, you will find high absenteeism, tardiness, accidents, and other problems that affect productivity. Alcohol does affect the entire body and mind as well as the pocketbook.

Nationwide studies indicate that alcohol, more than any other drug, is closely associated with the characteristics of violence and aggression. One study showed that children who had been physically abused or neglected were five times more likely to report alcohol abuse. Of all the rape cases in America, alcohol is involved in over half of them. Substance abuse brings out the worst in people, and we all will become victims in one way of another, be it physical, spiritual, or financial.

Many will reply, "Oh, I don't drink all that much. I am just what you call 'a social drinker.'" You feel justified with such rationalization. These infamous words demonstrate what is being said about the negative effect of alcohol on one's better judgment. The habit is depleting your financial resources—if nothing less. Any drinking that causes a problem—whether social, medical, spiritual, or financial—

mild or severe, is significant for prevention and treatment.

All of that notwithstanding, you will never start or maintain a tin can as long as you allow alcohol to absorb your finances. If you are a drinker, God wants to deliver you. In Hebrews 4:15–16 it says, "For we have not an high priest which cannot be touched with the feeling of our infirmities, but was in all points tempted like as we are, yet without sin. Let us therefore come boldly unto the throne of grace, that we may obtain mercy, and find grace to help in time of need."

I beg you to get delivered from this addiction if you are consuming alcohol. If you are not a partaker of this drug, that is great. If you know of a friend or family member who is, take note from their actions and do not allow yourself to become entangled into this web. Remember: The safest and most preventive method involving any and all drugs or addictions is *abstinence*—**A**ll **B**anishment **S**ecures **T**he **I**ndividual's **N**ullification, **E**xpressing **N**o **C**ompromising **E**ver.

Now I want to show you what you will have available to begin saving immediately (after you honor God with your firstfruits). Begin your tin can savings if you just received Jesus into your heart or received deliverance from alcohol.

ALCOHOL, YOUR COST!

The following statistics gathered from the fiscal years of 1995 and 1996 show that alcohol cost you $429 during that period—even if you didn't buy any!* Your money covered the costs of lost work time, lower productivity, higher health care, and extra hospitalization. I didn't buy any and you probably didn't either. Nevertheless, we paid for it. Yep, $429! Maybe it's all right with you, but it's not with me. I didn't attend the party. I wasn't invited. So why should I pay? Suppose we paid $429 per year for the last five years. That is a whopping $2,145 plus interest that we have lost!*

This is even more astounding for those of us who don't even drink! This could have gone toward your child's

---

* Statistics supplied by the Center for Substance Abuse Prevention and Mental Health Services Administration. Others from the National Clearinghouse for Alcohol and Drug Information. Publications catalog, Fall/Winter, 1990-1996. U.S. Department of Health and Human Services.

Building Wealth Using the Tin Can Method

educational savings. It could have been your wife's new kitchen or your family's vacation that you never got to take.

Americans pay $112 billion each year on alcohol abuse. And that's just part of the cost. Emotional, social, and family hardships also take their toll. Learn what you can do to prevent alcohol and drug abuse problems before they start.

Take a look at what a moderate "problem" drinker spends in addition to government "contributions" to alcohol consumption:

BEER
(Based on *two* quarts per day at $1.40 per quart.)

WEEK	WEEKLY SUBTOTAL	TOTAL
WEEK #1	Monday–$2.80	
	Tuesday–$2.80	
	Wednesday–$2.80	
	Thursday–$2.80	
	Friday–$2.80	
	Saturday–$2.80	
	Sunday$2.80	
	Weekly Total $19.60	$19.60
WEEK #2	$19.60	$39.20
WEEK #3	$19.60	$58.80
WEEK #4	$19.60	$78.40

One month of drinking two quarts of beer per day at $1.40 per quart equals $78.40.

One year of drinking two quarts of beer per day at $1.40 per quart equals $940.80.

DO YOU HAVE $940.80 IN A SAVINGS ACCOUNT?

No, the beer companies have it. Have these companies made a donation to your favorite charity or to your church lately? Probably not. And they won't. They're probably basking in the sun on the Cayman Islands with a chilled

Excusers, Abusers, and Misusers

beer can in their hands and their pockets bulging with your $940.80—and the $940.80 of each of millions of people just like you.

For them the sky's the limit. What about you?

(Based on *three* quarts per day at $1.40 per quart except Sundays)

WEEK	WEEKLY SUBTOTAL		TOTAL
WEEK #1	Monday–$4.20		
	Tuesday–$4.20		
	Wednesday–$4.20		
	Thursday–$4.20		
	Friday–$4.20		
	Saturday–$4.20		
	Weekly Total	$25.20	$25.20
WEEK #2		$25.20	$50.40
WEEK #3		$25.20	$75.60
WEEK #4		$25.20	$100.80

One month of drinking three quarts of beer per day at $1.40 per quart equals $100.80.

One year of drinking three quarts of beer per day at $1.40 per quart equals $1,209.60.

NOW, DO YOU HAVE $1,209.60 IN A SAVINGS ACCOUNT?

I invite you to pray the following prayer with me:

> *Father God, forgive me for my numerous sins—especially alcohol use. Come into my heart. Deliver and save me. Help me to do what I cannot do alone. I detest this alcohol addiction. You are a God of miracles. I need a miracle now. Cleanse me from the top to the bottom and from the inside and out. Thank You for what You have done for me. In Your Son Jesus' name, I ask and I count it done. Amen.*

Building Wealth Using the Tin Can Method

God is not a liar, His Word will not return unto Him void. Write me so that I too may rejoice in victory with you. Here's to your health and wealth!

Think About It—
You won't have to fake it if you don't take it—but if you take it, you certainly can't fake it—for it shows!

The Stinking Cost of Tobacco

The U.S. Surgeon General issued a report in 1989 that emphatically concluded that cigarettes and other forms of tobacco are addicting. Nicotine is the drug in tobacco that causes addiction. The report also determined that smoking was a major cause of death in the United States. Nevertheless, a national household survey on drug abuse recently reported that some fifty million Americans continue to smoke cigarettes, making nicotine one of the most addictive drugs in the United States.

Don't be fooled or naive. Nicotine is a transitory stimulant and a sedative to the central nervous system. The intake of nicotine results in an immediate "kick" because it evokes a discharge of epinephrine. *Epinephrine* is a hormone that stimulates heart action and increases blood pressure from the adrenal cortex located near the kidneys. This stimulates the central nervous system. Stimulation is followed by depression and fatigue, and this entices the abuser to seek and use more nicotine.

Since 1975, cigarettes have consistently been the substance most frequently used on a daily basis by high school students, including many in the church. No wonder it's a billion-dollar industry! And no wonder Satan has such a big stake in this industry! One desire of Satan's is to channel finances from God's kingdom in order to finance his own.

And every time one buys a pack of Joe Camels, a contribution has been made. Not only that, but Satan can double the trouble by wiping out millions through sickness and disease that will lead to death and the unfulfilled destinies of many. Smoking will take your *health* and your *wealth* away.

THINK ABOUT IT—
PEOPLE BETWEEN THE AGES OF TWENTY-SIX AND THIRTY-FOUR HAVE THE HIGHEST RATES OF SMOKING AND PROBABLY THE LOWEST PERCENTAGE OF SAVINGS.

A pack of cigarettes today isn't cheap. And the price keeps going up. If you are a smoker, and you say you can't save, the following chart will show you how much would be possible by giving up the habit. God will help you do it if you truly desire to stop.

THE COST OF SMOKING CIGARETTES
(All amounts are based on two packs per day at a cost of $1.75 a pack.)

WEEK	WEEKLY SUBTOTAL		TOTAL
WEEK #1	Monday–$3.50		
	Tuesday–$3.50		
	Wednesday–$3.50		
	Thursday–$3.50		
	Friday–$3.50		
	Saturday–$3.50		
	Sunday$3.50		
	Weekly Total	$24.50	$24.50
WEEK #2	$24.50		$49.00
WEEK #3	$24.50		$73.50
WEEK #4	$24.50		$98.00

Building Wealth Using the Tin Can Method

One month of cigarettes equals $98.00.
One year of cigarettes equals $1,176.00.
DO YOU HAVE $1,176.00 IN A SAVINGS ACCOUNT? NO! IT HAS ALL GONE UP IN SMOKE!

CIGARETTES
(Based on two cartons a week at $15.50 per carton.)

WEEK	WEEKLY SUBTOTAL	TOTAL
WEEK #1	$31.00	$31.00
WEEK #2	$31.00	$62.00
WEEK #3	$31.00	$93.00
WEEK #4	$31.00	$124.00

One month of cigarettes equals $124.00.
One year of cigarettes equals $1,488.00.
DO YOU HAVE $1,488.00 IN A SAVINGS ACCOUNT?

Of course, one-pack-a-day smokers would pay half of that amount yearly ($744.00). And three-pack-a-day smokers (which is not uncommon) would pay half as much more ($2,232.00).

Staggering, isn't it? Mind blowing! Yet you many of you who smoke won't give God the 10 percent that belongs to Him. It's His goodness and mercy that has kept you alive today!

But this is just the financial reality. Here are a few more hazards to your health and wealth to consider as you make your daily contributions to Satan's kingdom and plan:

- Nicotine escalates bronchial disorders.
- Nicotine increases the risk of congestive heart failure.
- Nicotine affects the moods as well as the heart, lungs, and stomach.
- Nicotine can produce sweating, vomiting, and throat irritation.

- Nicotine is associated with cancer of the esophagus, mouth, lips, and larynx.
- Nicotine can increase the risk among pregnant women of still births and premature infants.
- Women nicotine users generally experience menopause earlier. Using nicotine will rob you of all your pennies and deny your tin can savings.

Not only that, but the Environmental Protection Agency recently concluded that "secondhand" smoke causes lung cancer in nonsmoking adults and greatly increases the risk of respiratory illnesses in children. Smokers are spreading Satan's kingdom around regardless of who wants to contribute!

Because there are many more Christians who smoke than drink (I believe), I need to stay on this one a bit longer. Who are you to stand before almighty God and say, "I can't afford to give to the gospel, but I can afford to slowly kill myself?" Who are you to stand before Him and complain that you aren't being blessed enough to save, yet you were blessed enough with your job. Yes, the job you maintain presently to finance this ugly, stinking habit. Satan doesn't love you. He's incapable of love. He's a destroyer of your soul and body, if you let him. He lures people into these nasty habits and then tells them nothing will hurt them. "Oh, yes," he lies, "the others may smoke themselves into the grave, but not you." He comes to kill, steal, and destroy. And he's destroying your spirit and sound judgment. Tell him right now, "Enough is enough, you stinker! I've had it with you!" Your tin can is waiting, too.

As with all addictions, deliverance is available. There are many smoke-banishing products on the market if you need help aids to cease smoking. However, the great I AM is the master helper. He is your deliverer if you trust Him and truly desire to be set free.

Here's a prayer for deliverance:

> *Father, I have been a smoker for a long time. I allowed myself to be deceived by Satan, but no more. I ask You to come into my heart and my life, Jesus. Deliver me from this addiction. Cleanse me thoroughly. Make me brand new. Set me free from this bondage that I may live and obey Your Word. Thank You for not judging me. Thank You for accepting me. Thank You for setting me free. I am now free, free in Jesus' name. Amen.*

Sit down and take a few minutes of your time to write me. I and millions of others are standing with you in prayer. Remember, God is your deliverer. Glory to His name. Here's to your health and wealth, the tin can way.

THINK ABOUT IT—
IF AN AVERAGE PERSON GAMBLES, DRINKS, AND SMOKES, KNOW FOR A SURETY THAT HE'S DEFINITELY BROKE— AND THOUSANDS DO.

Once you quit smoking, you can help finance the gospel and save $744, $1,448, or $2,232 in your tin can! Get right. Get in order with God's plan for your life. He's a redeemer of the time. He will start you out anew and will accelerate your prosperity and put you on a path toward true happiness in Him. Glory to His name!

Fast Food

Now, how about your lunch habits? If you are a fast-food restaurant lunch junkie who zips your car in and out of pick-up windows or rushes in and out on foot, here is another opportunity to start your tin can. When you see the following figures, you may be shocked to learn how much you are paying these fast-food chains every day. And you

Excusers, Abusers, and Misusers

may just be inspired to start rerouting this money into your tin can as a nightly ritual as you pack your lunch. In fact, I recommend it!

DAILY LUNCH AT MCBURGERS

(All amounts are based on hamburger, fries, and drink at a total of $5 per day for six days.)

WEEK	WEEKLY SUBTOTAL		TOTAL
WEEK #1	Monday–$5.00		
	Tuesday–$5.00		
	Wednesday–$5.00		
	Thursday–$5.00		
	Friday–$5.00		
	Saturday$5.00		
	Weekly Total	$30.00	$30.00
WEEK #2		$30.00	$60.00
WEEK #3		$30.00	$90.00
WEEK #4		$30.00	$120.00

One month of fast-food lunches at $5 per day equals $120.
One year of fast-food lunches at $5 per day equals $1,440.
DO YOU HAVE $1,440.00 IN A SAVINGS ACCOUNT?

THE PSYCHIC PHENOMENON CRAZE

There's much that can be said concerning today's popular psychic craze. Christian and non-Christians alike are seeking this money-abusive deception of television's new guru psychics.

About this social phenomenon, let me just say this: There is more to these "fortunetellers" than mere entertainment, and the truth of the matter is, this type of entertainment doesn't come cheap. I do hope one wouldn't consider $3.99

BUILDING WEALTH USING THE TIN CAN METHOD

a minute as being cheap or just chunk change. It's certainly not chunk change after five or ten minutes ($3.99 x 10 minutes = $39.90). Now it becomes hunk change. A few breaths or blinks and a minute has escaped.

Believe it or not, some acquaintances of mine who are employed by various telephone companies related to me that millions and millions of dollars are being spent by people calling these psychic networks. They said some bills exceeded hundreds and thousands of dollars per customer. One acquaintance of mine recalled one person who spends $400 a month in phone bills, and another who spent $5,000 by calling the psychic network repeatedly. When my friend asked the person who spent the $400 why the phone bill was so high, the person told her it was because of her search for a mate.

Many of you are seeking romance and finance via ignorance. Many find it easier to seek and pay psychics for guidance than to seek God and pay nothing for His advice. His Word tells you everything—and you can bank on its truth. "Call upon me, and I'll answer thee and show you great and mighty things which you knowest not" (Jer. 33:3).

Take a look at the following chart that illustrates the money many people today are spending on such psychic "hot lines." There are many people that spend even more money on psychics than our chart indicates.

CALLS TO THE PSYCHIC NETWORK
(Based on a rate of $3.99 per minute.)

DAY	MINUTES	TOTAL
Week #1		
Monday	5	$19.95
Wednesday	5	19.95
Friday	5	19.95
TOTAL FOR 3 DAYS		**$59.85**

DAY	MINUTES	TOTAL
Week #2		
Tuesday	5	$19.95
Thursday	5	19.95
Friday	7	27.93
Sunday	10	39.90
TOTAL FOR 4 DAYS		**$107.73**
Week #3		
Tuesday	5	$19.95
Thursday	10	39.90
Friday	6	23.94
TOTAL FOR 3 DAYS		**$83.79**
Week #4		
Monday	10	$39.90
Saturday	10	39.90
TOTAL FOR 2 DAYS		**$79.80**
TOTAL FOR THE MONTH		**$331.17**

Note #1: During week #4 this person traveled out of town to visit relatives. Relatives would not allow calls to the psychic network.

Note #2: This month represents $331.17 worth of funds for fun! These funds should have been placed in your tin can savings.

God has a dynamic telephone communication service unlike anything AT&T, MCI, Sprint, or any other could imagine. Everyone in this entire world can call and talk with Him *at the same time without an overload.* God is in the "show me" business. He'll give you the answer with the proof to follow that will be everlasting and 100 percent accurate. It won't cost you $3.99 a minute—and the time of day you choose to talk with Him is unlimited. He'll listen all day and night if you choose.

The world's fortunetellers are seeking to make a fortune

off you. God does not operate in this manner. James 1:5 says, "If any of you lack wisdom, let him ask of God, that giveth to all men liberally [for free], and upbraideth not; and it shall be given him." God is a God of generosity. **He is not—and will not be—in the fortune "telling" and "selling" business.**

You wouldn't think I'd have to mention this in a Christian-oriented book. But I know there are many Christians who get suckered into these psychic hot lines. Satan wants you to believe in him. And in order for you to believe in psychics, they must show you some evidence of their track record. In other words, they must show you their "so-called" *good* side.

What does the enemy do? He lures you by a familiar spirit. A spirit that's just familiar enough with you to tell you something about yourself that you feel it shouldn't know under normal circumstances. And because of this, thousands are getting hooked. Psychics gain your confidence, trust, and faithfulness carefully—then comes the boom!

Soon you're lured into an entrapment that may very well cost you or a loved one dearly later on. What a person spends on their telephone bills could have been saved to put into the work of the gospel. Your tin can money and, most importantly, God's portion, would have yielded you much more by now—and in more ways than pouring it into the devil's lap.

So, here it is. Here is your nice $5,000 beginning for your investment portfolio or a down payment on a house or a piece of property. You could use it for your child's educational money so that you won't have to borrow money and pay it back with interest. Or buy some new furniture for the redecorating of your home or a new car, paid for in full, without having to take a loan with hefty interest from the finance company. Maybe $5,000 represents that long-prayed-for-and-sought-after vacation for you or your family.

Say these words aloud:

I can save; I will save! I will not miss out on what God is going to do. I will ge in order, I will get ready. I will help finance the End-Time harvest!

Sneaker Rich, Savings Poor

Let's look at some unnecessary expenditures that aren't "health endangering," but they are detrimental to our common sense. Destinies have been denied to many of our youths due to the senseless killing over certain name-brand sneakers or tennis shoes. Sneakers are a billion-dollar industry geared toward today's youth via TV commercials, newspaper ads, and billboards. And they aren't cheap by any means. Many famous athletes are paid a fortune just for their names to appear on certain some brands.

It is to these athletes that I now appeal. You see, the prestige of wearing a famous, athletic brand of sneakers for many youths evokes an outlandish sense of pride and self-worth. Many refuse to attend school unless their parents invest in a pair for their wardrobe. And believe it or not, many parents are ulcer-oriented and stressed out from maintaining second jobs to afford these luxury sneakers.

Some of these parents live in undesirable conditions and surroundings with little hope for their future, yet they manage to come up with the $100 plus that it costs to buy these items. Not only that, but this billion-dollar-plus industry takes much out of communities and puts very little back. So, simply STOP! Take a stand, without wearing those sneakers. And share your stand with others, to stop the madness.

Stop the Madness

To the shoe industry and famous athletes who are profiting from this madness, I say, where is your concern for the youths who are our future? What example are you setting

BUILDING WEALTH USING THE TIN CAN METHOD

for them? Do you even care? Yes, I know they and their parents have the distinct choice to purchase them or not. But everywhere they turn, on cereal boxes and various other cartons, you're constantly flashing your signature brand before their faces. You have calculated their every move. Your ads and marketing strategies say, "Here we are, you must have us. Your parents must work extra jobs in order for you to wear our foreign-made foot coverings at a hundred dollars a pair!"

Parents, many athletic stars and superstars care little about your child. They only care about you and your child's money. Many have given little or no thought to the threat their athletic products may pose to the welfare of your children.

So again, stop it. Don't continue to allow your children to become *sneaker rich and savings poor.* Stop the madness of allowing them to wear $100+ sneakers while you show a zero balance in your savings account. **I dare say that if many would take a dollar assessment of the sneakers in their children's closets, they would find well over a thousand dollars buried in canvas and rubber.** I see and hear many parents in deep concern, mentally laboring about how they will afford to send their children to college. I wonder if it would have been less worrisome if they had exercised more restraint from the purchasing of expensive sneakers for their child.

Let's add it up. Let's say each school term, from kindergarten to high school, $200 was spent on a child for sneakers. That would estimate to be about $400 a year times twelve years, totaling over $4,800 that could have been invested in a savings. Yet that same family never thought of saving or encouraging their sneaker-rich child to save that amount every year. Time passes so rapidly that before you know it, little Johnny or Susie has grown from the crib to high school graduation. And when it is time for college, out of desperation many parents are forced to take out student loans, throwing themselves and their children

Excusers, Abusers, and Misusers

into debt, with the interest constantly accruing. It becomes even more problematic if job finding becomes difficult after college graduation, prolonging the indebtedness and the accumulating interest.

Do you get the picture of what could occur if you or someone you know who has been caught in the sneaker trap would make a decision to stop the madness? I realize there are many money-snatching culprits out there trying to hurl their overpriced javelins of greed into us and our kids. But the sneaker industry somehow seems to be a national forerunner in this prestige-greed market.

Are you ready for one final chart? This one will show you where the rubber meets the road.

SNEAKER RICH, SAVINGS POOR SURVEY CHART

BRAND	COST
Air Jordan	$150 average
Nike	$180 average
Fila	$89 average
Reebok	$125 average
Adidas	$89 average
Converse	$89 average

These prices vary depending upon the store and area of purchase.

Most kids purchase four or more pairs of sneakers each year. Stop the madness. Talk to your children. Start a sneaker college fund and release them from this FAD.

CAR MENTALITY—COUNT THE COST!

Finally, it's been said that it's hard to teach an old dog new tricks, so start when your children are young. Once we get in order, we must impart our wisdom to get our kids in order. Parents fuss all the time, saying, "I just gave you $50 yesterday; you should have saved some of it." But we really don't have any example on which to base this kind of statement because we usually haven't taught them about money or how to save. Kids don't respect money because we don't respect money. So as you learn, teach them, because they must learn to respect the value of a dollar.

What Savings Poor Young Adults Drive

MODEL	ESTIMATED PRICE	MODEL	ESTIMATED PRICE
Jaguar	$70,000+	Nissan/240	$18,000+
Mercedes Benz	$60,000+	Lexus Sedan	$38,000+
Audi	$30,000+	Mazda RX7	$18,000+
BMW	$40,000+	Nissan Pathfinder	$32,000+
Jeep	$24,000+	Ford Explorer	$24,000+
Camaro	$22,000+	Toyota Camry	$22,000+
Truck	$15,000+		

Prices may vary based upon area and dealership.

The Value of a Dollar

When your children are old enough to drive, help them understand finances through the purchase of a car. This item is a money guzzler, so it can be used more than any other early financial experience to teach them dollars and cents.

Many kids haven't been trained up in the ways of financial understanding and accountability. They have no idea of the true value of money.

Children think as they are led to believe. If a parent doesn't take the time to sit down and explain the rip-off involved in paying $150 for sneakers and other popularized apparel that "all the kids are wearing," that child won't recognize the importance of one dollar. And this could really

Excusers, Abusers, and Misusers

get serious when it's time to buy a car. The car industry gets very interested in your child's money when he or she is old enough to drive. And they take it upon themselves to teach and train your child in what is and isn't good—so you better be there when they get that part-time job.

The average sixteen- to twenty-three-year-old will purchase a used car at $5,000, then turn around and install high-tech audio equipment worth at least $500 in the depreciating vehicle. The equipment won't appreciate the car, and that same child will want to drain any savings you have inspired them to accumulate (if they even have a savings account) to "properly" equip their vehicle.

As a parent, you may be saying, "As long as they're working and paying for these items, why should we care? It's not coming out of our pockets! The kid has a job, so let him make and spend his money the way he wants! What's wrong with that? It's not coming out of our pockets."

Let me caution you, something will eventually be coming out of your pockets, because sooner or later your child's ignorance will catch up with you. And when it does, they will turn to you for help. When the child suffers, so do the parents. A once manageable car payment could end up costing $400 a month with all the gidget McGadgets they put into their car if you co-sign for a loan. Once every penny they have is going to finance their new set of wheels, they will be turning to you to pick up the slack. And this in turn could lead them to believe they will always have a place to turn, for someone to pick up the slack, like finance companies and credit cards.

The solution is simple. We should never give our kids any item without first training or teaching them about that item. Remember, a fool and his money are quickly parted. So get out the financial sheets and facts regarding any purchase; show them how much the addition of any accessories will truly add to the value of the car; ask them how they will work to make up any difference; and use this particularly high-priced item as a true financial training tool during their teenage years.

For example, a Ford Escort is classified as an inexpensive vehicle for a young adult's first car purchase. It would average a monthly payment of $190. But when accessories are added it could escalate their total monthly cost into a higher bracket through a finance company.

The child could actually end up with a monthly payment of $600 on a $10,000 car. This is sick. Point all of these things out, and you will be teaching them to deal with other financial matters. As life goes on, people get into all types of financial bondage just to purchase that new "shiny thing" to park in their yard as a showpiece. Do you realize how many people are forfeiting their family life because of working two and three jobs, just to meet the payments on their car, or cars?

It is these same people who encourage their children to save for a new car instead of something really important such as future building through savings, a monetary pledge to the house of God, or their education so it won't be a strain and burden when college time arrives. Many young adults are in college today with an educational loan accruing interest that is awaiting their graduation to welcome them into the world of DEBT.

So when you get in order, get your children in order. Teach them to enter God's giving contest. Teach them to honor God with their firstfruits and to pay themselves. Then teach them to use the balance of their money for shopping. In this way, the gospel will be financed; God will prove His love by giving them the increase; and they will be able to share God's principles of finance with their children.

> Suppose one of you wants to build a tower. Will he not first sit down and estimate the cost to see if he has enough money to complete it?
>
> —LUKE 14:28

Eleven
A Tin Can for the Rich and Famous?

When God impressed me to write this book, there were a number of initial hindering thoughts and factors that detained me. They were:

1. The devil didn't want me to write it.

2. I felt that everything that could be said about finances had been said.

3. I felt no one cared or even wanted to hear about finances anymore.

4. I didn't believe I was qualified, even though I had over twenty years of trial-and-error experience that qualified me.

5. And finally, I didn't want to be ridiculed by my peers.

But more than any of these hindering thoughts, I was mainly embarrassed about the title, *Building Wealth Using the Tin Can Method,* because I didn't think a tin can was representative of my personal style or taste—a silk purse, but certainly not a tin can. Nevertheless, I overcame these hesitancies eventually, because I was once in the same boat with most of my readers—including the rich and famous.

Lifestyles of the Rich and Famous

As I was sitting by the window in my living room five years ago, God clearly impressed in my spirit how the rich and famous need to hear about the tin can method, too. I began to argue, and I said within myself, *God, these people are rich. I can't embarrass myself by saying to them, "Even though you make millions of dollars, many of you don't have an adequate savings." I can't tell them that they fall into the same category of ordinary salaried folks in their finances. Can you see them perched in their sprawling homes amid their beautiful luxuries when I bring up the tin can method?*

Then my thoughts began to subside, and the telephone rang. It was a very dear friend of mine who was once married to a famous actor. I hadn't spoken to her in years. It was through our conversation that I was finally convinced that this book would not only be for the masses of what we term "ordinary, everyday, working people," but that it would be for the "elite" as well. It would be as much for the rich and famous as it is for the blue-collar workers. It would be for anyone who isn't obeying God's ordinances and walking in divine order.

My friend and I began to talk about many things concerning our children and other details of our lives. But we said nothing about finances as we talked. Then, just as we were about to say our good- byes and hang up, she made a comment about a financial matter. She began to talk about something about which the Lord and I had just mentally dialogued. Talk about goose bumps! The hairs on my arms began to stand tall as the tin can method and message were being confirmed in my spirit again.

I told her about my book and its message, and she stayed on the line with great interest. The importance of this conversation showed that she believed the message, and that she and her spouse had been a victim of rejecting the principles of God's order. I am telling you her story in her own words, because the problems her family experienced should speak to other wealthy families in the hope that they will heed and divert the sting of their loss.

My friend's story:

"Our friends were those rich and glamorous people you watch on television and see in the movies. They were also the outspoken politicians whom you trust to represent you in Washington. You view them as the world's richest, most beautiful people, living perfect lives in a fantasy world you wish you could call your own. You are sure you would be happy if you could attain just a little of what they have.

"Well, I am here to wake you up from your dream and bring you back to reality. The image you have of these public personalities has been created in your own minds, with a lot of help from the media.

"If you lived behind the scenes you would realize they are some of the most miserable and unhappy people in the world. Their smiles deceive you and hide the pain they must keep secret in order to keep that image alive. After all, it's what you expect.

"How do I know? I know because I was one of them and lived the same lifestyle. I was under the pressure of having to maintain a false image every time I stepped outside my door. At the most unhappy and hurtful time in my life, we were being filmed for a segment of *Lifestyles of the Rich and Famous*. This was supposed to be the most wonderful and happy time of my life, yet behind my smile were tears.

"Why?...you ask...could someone with seemingly everything be so unhappy? The answer is quite simple. Our lives didn't line up with God's order. And when something is out of order it is broken down.

"You could see we weren't a typical family. Everyone on the outside looking in thought we had it made. We even thought we had it made. We were in a financial position to have just about anything our hearts desired. So, we spent foolishly on the things we desired. We bought those things that gave us pleasure, rather than prioritizing what we needed as a family to make a stable home for our children and us. We weren't good stewards of the blessings God had entrusted us with.

"We should have sat down together as a couple and made a list of priorities, *with God being the #1 priority*. However, there was no thought given to what we wanted to achieve. We had no plan, no goals, and no time schedule—which equals no order. We had no plan for the future and thought only of the moment. Knowing that life holds no guarantee of what tomorrow might bring made no difference. So there was no consideration as to what would happen to us if the river of flowing cash were to dry up.

"God never intended for His children to be in debt. Maxed-out credit cards, unpaid bills, and owing family and friends money because of foolish spending (especially with our income) was not His plan for us. We are expected to prioritize the necessities first. To do otherwise, is a discredit to God and ourselves. And what a terrible example to set for our children! Remember, they watch what we do more than listen to what we say. So when they become undisciplined and unstructured adults who spend out of control, we must blame ourselves for not teaching them the correct and proper way.

"Let me share a few examples of how we didn't prioritize our life or necessities. God should have been our first financial obligation as we gave back to Him what was rightfully His. Then, usually, the first consideration a couple makes is for a home. So a roof over your head should be priority #2. But in our case my spouse was not interested in a home.

He was impatient and into instant gratification. He wanted the "cars" of his dreams. And whatever he wanted was what he got. After all, he was the head of the home, he had control, and he wanted to have fun.

"Unfortunately, as Dr. James Dobson best says it, 'The motive for family disintegration is nothing more substantial than *unbridled selfishness.*' So we paid exorbitant amounts of money for rent on a house we would never own.

"Another way money was wasted was on exotic vacations. One vacation a year wasn't enough. So we spent tens of thousands of dollars four or five times a year traveling to the Caribbean, Hawaii, or some other exotic place. On top of that we paid all the expenses of certain friends who tagged along. But of course that was a part of keeping up the image of being a jet-setter.

"Our paradise became a parched desert with no water, and I was thirsty. I was surrounded by people, and yet, so lonely. I was the happiest when I was alone at home when taking solitary walks that allowed me to reflect on the beauty of God's creation. And I was finding more and more comfort while privately studying God's Word.

"I began to retreat into my own world and discovered the meaning of order. God blessed me with a book called *Honest to God.* I was impressed with the section that dealt with finances, which instructed the payment of God's 10 percent tithe, and then another 10 percent payment of savings to ourselves. I put the formula into practice, and it worked! Working with my monthly allowance, which was almost nothing, I soon had close to $15,000 saved. I know that may seem like a pittance to many who share our status. And it really wasn't very much, considering the amount of money that was coming into the household. But after falling and becoming financially poor, $15,000 was a lot.

"It was so exciting to watch my savings grow. So exciting, in fact, that I found myself cutting back on the little extras so I could save more. But the closer I came to putting my life in order, the further apart my spouse and I grew. Ultimately, he left me, and a downward chain of events began to take place. His fame waned, his image tarnished, and the river of flowing cash dried up. When he walked out, I was devastated. I was suddenly displaced. There I was in my forties with no job, no skills, and no money. I was scared.

"Even though our priorities had been out of order, I never had to worry about finances. There had been plenty of money. But after we separated, there was no money coming in, and I didn't own anything. The house I lived in was not my own. The car I drove was not paid for, and I no longer had medical coverage. These were just a few of the necessities of life, not to mention the loss of the lavish lifestyle that my children and I had grown accustomed to.

"As I lay across my bed in a pool of tears one day, I realized I was neglecting my children and that wallowing in self-pity wasn't helping anyone. I remember my favorite Bible verse and clung to it: 'I will never leave you, nor forsake you.' My faith in God was strong, and I knew that even though I had to start over with a new beginning, He would walk beside me as I put His order into my life. And He has, all thanks to God!

"I strongly suggest to men and women, rich and poor, famous and nonfamous, to live a life of God's order. Because He said, 'Obedience is better than sacrifice.' And, it is so.

"I hope by sharing my story you may find comfort in knowing you are not alone, even after you fail. There is hope because of God's great mercy. You can begin again, right now—today. God bless you."

People, all people, great and small, need God. I realize now that just because one is rich doesn't mean they are also wise. Just because your talent allows you to make millions doesn't mean you're wise enough to keep it—or to live long enough to fully enjoy it.

A Tin Can for the Rich and Famous?

Recall the Old Testament figure Nabal in 1 Samuel 25. He was rich, but the Word implies he also was a fool. He disrespected David and was disobedient with what the Lord had empowered him to amass. He wouldn't share or give to God's chosen and anointed vessel, David. In fact, Nabal was a classic example of a hoarder.

So what happened to Nabal? He died and forfeited all he had, including his wife, Abigail, whom David later married. He was a lousy steward of what God had blessed him with. Yes, he was rich, but he certainly was far from being wise.

Up and Down Lifestyles of the Rich and Famous

I am appalled and amazed at many of our professional athletes, singers, actors, musicians, actresses, businessmen, talk show hosts, and others who are rich and on top today—but penniless and down-trodden tomorrow. Remember, success for some comes suddenly, literally overnight. And in many cases their success escapes them just as suddenly—overnight.

> **THINK ABOUT IT—**
> HOW MANY TIMES HAVE YOU SEEN OR HEARD OF THE WEALTH, HOUSES, FLEET OF CARS, CLOTHING, OR OTHER PERSONAL BELONGINGS OF CELEBRITIES BEING AUCTIONED FOR A SMALL FRACTION OF THEIR ORIGINAL COST?

When you haven't been taught early to respect God's financial road that leads to a successful financial future, you will certainly capture the "spirit of loss" in your life. It will visit you, mingle with you, and eventually take everything you have away from you.

For some, foolish losses come from activities such as gambling, drugs, drinking, or an overexuberant lifestyle.

Building Wealth Using the Tin Can Method

They never think to invest or save for the possibility of loss of work due to health problems or the loss of their job. This applies especially to actors and actresses who may be in great demand one year, but out of demand the next few years. Unless they have been wise with their spending habits and upscale lifestyles, they may find themselves losing everything—and experiencing the heartache of rejection in their spirit as well.

Many athletes have had to give up the very sport they loved because of an unexpected injury, accident, or some other physical mishap. Celebrities, Wall Street workers, investors, and athletes lose all they have because of an out-of-control drug, gambling, or party habit. Many experience financial ruin through divorce and promiscuous lifestyles.

It only takes one heavy-duty circumstance to bring anyone down, such as we recently witnessed in the O. J. Simpson case. Even the ugly system of the IRS can hurl its spears of poverty into your life. I recall the situation that surrounded Sammy Davis, Jr., Leona Hensley, and Red Foxx, and I'm sure numerous others that we may or may not have heard about. These people were living on knob and snob hill one day, and were suddenly on their way down hill the next. Much money was made, but very little saved.

People magazine contained an article in its October 7, 1996, issue written by Emily Mitchell and Ken Baker that dealt with "Those Left Behind." The article talked about Ray Combes, who was forty years old when he was replaced on the TV show *Family Feud* in 1994 by the original host, Richard Dawson. The article stated that Mr. Combes was earning close to $1 million a year, but that he was drowning in debt. He owed nearly $500,000, including $100,000 in back taxes, and close to $150,000 in loans and credit cards. His businesses had failed, and he owed another $470,000 mortgage on his five-bedroom Glendale home. A friend stated that he wasn't very good at managing money.

Tragically, the article continued, Mr. Combes took his life because of the pressures and strains of his financial situation.

Sometimes embarrassment and shame are all that is left from a once-successful life. There are no guarantees that you will bounce back tomorrow. You never regain your momentum. And sometimes, family and loved ones are left behind to bear the burden, as was the case with the wife and six children of Ray Combes.

It seems to me that there are also many successful athletes who put the "cart before the horse" today when they strike it rich. After one signs those million-dollar contracts, it would make a lot of sense to lay aside some money for a seminar on money management. But instead, most go out and buy a multimillion dollar home, four or five cars, and huge gifts and parties for family and friends.

Now don't get me wrong, I don't have a problem with anyone purchasing such big-ticket items. But there are many celebrity athletes and stars who come out of poverty with little or no financial knowledge to help them manage their money. Many of them don't know God or His financial blueprint. And you know the devourer is there when they sign those contracts, smacking his lips, waiting to pounce. Take the time to enroll in a financial seminar, buy this book, or even give me a call—and let's get your adverse financial condition turned around.

Remember: The horse always goes before the cart to lead it where it's supposed to go. No one is exempt from the devourer when they're out of order. When you are in the arena of the lifestyle of the rich and famous, you could come up against one lawsuit that could strip you of everything except the bare necessities. One wrong word spoken or one wrong step taken can sometimes birth the ugliest lawsuit of your life. Even if you win the case, there are money-hungry lawyers out there who want to strip you of the rest of your millions.

Building Wealth Using the Tin Can Method

What I am trying to get across to you is that we all need the Lord. We need His accurate plan for our lives and our finances. In those times when troubles arise, we can feel secure about going boldly to His throne of grace to ask for help (Heb. 4:16). We will have the favor of God on our side when we are in order. He miraculously provides the most ingenious ways of escape. But if we aren't obedient, Satan and his pack of devouring vultures can have a field day with us.

Remember, riches don't make anyone exempt from the devourer. Neither wealth or fame means anything to Satan when you are out of order. It just means he has a greater quantity to dive into when he takes all. Granted, it may take him more time to get to you through it, but you certainly don't intimidate him. He is a master in using creative and manipulative approaches. When you are in order, however, God will fight and win your battles.

God is not against your having things. He is against things having you. God isn't against riches; He is against out-of-order living. The gifts and abilities you have to make money came from Him: "Every good gift is from above" (James 1:17). So this certainly warrants your putting Him first.

Satan has exploited and received into his pocket too much of what God has blessed you with. Remember, "A fool and his money are soon parted." So seek knowledge and go after God's financial order. It will save you a lot of headache, hardship, and pain. When trouble arises, God will show up on your behalf. Don't allow yourself or your family to suffer because of foolishness. All the money you have belongs to God anyway. He only asks that you give Him a tenth *first*. Don't let a million-dollar home become more important than your priceless God.

Accountability Is Calling You

Accountability is calling to the "rich and famous." Will you answer? Will you be obedient and do what God has commanded? What you do with your finances determines whom you love and serve. Get in order, put God first, pay yourself next, then pay your bills. Then after all of these things, the sky can be the limit—with panache.

Riches to Stitches

The key is putting God first. There are many in America today who have been blessed with hundreds, thousands, and even millions of dollars that they could give to the work of God. But there are many who won't even give fifty cents to the gospel! Surely, oh, rich one, you can't think this money is going to remain in your possession? The Bible states *clearly* that "the wealth of the wicked is laid up for the just" (Prov. 13:22). All the gold and silver belongs to God (Hag. 2:8). Did you not know that the earth is the Lord's and the fullness thereof (Ps. 24:1)? The Word also says that it is He (God) who gives us the power to get wealth and not we ourselves (Deut. 8:18).

Bearing all of this in mind, the apostle James wrote of the unrighteous rich man: "Come now, you rich, weep and howl for your miseries that are coming upon you!" (James 5:1, NKJV). God didn't say that miseries *may* come upon the selfish rich, He said *they shall come upon them.*

In 1997 the Arts and Entertainment (A&E) network aired a segment on the rich in America. At that time, there were 150 billionaires in this country according to their research. Some, I'm sure, are doing good and aiding their fellow Americans. However most are without form and void within their thinking, possessing no respect for the plight of others and God's sovereign order. They are swindlers of their inheritance on a grand scale. Where there is no respect and honor for God, there is usually no happiness with money, regardless of the amount of one's abundance.

The same responsibility that is attached to penance is attached to wealth. You must give back a due portion to insure a continuous flow. Let me say again that God is not against our having things (including money). What He is against is things having (controlling) us.

When and if "things" control or consume you, tragedy, unhappiness, misdirected obeisance, and poverty will follow you closely until you're consumed one way or another.

Take for instance, Barbara Hutton, from the rich and famous Woolworth family. She was left an inheritance worth $80 million. If money could ever buy anyone happiness, contentment, or peace, surely $80 million could do the job, right? But it can't, and it won't. Mrs. Hutton led a miserable life. She was rich, yet she was also poor. She lived the life of a super-rich heiress, yet the devourer never left her side. It is said that she had seven husbands, finding no contentment in any of them. And when she died, according to the A&E network's report, she had a meager $3,500 in the bank.

I hope the countless number of other filthy rich (as we have coined them) who are "sitting pretty" so to speak, will open their eyes to follow God's path to insure contentment within themselves and their lifestyle.

King Solomon's Riches

The richest man ever to walk the face of the earth was Israel's King Solomon, and his choices eventually ruined his heirs. His wealth was inherited from his father, King David.

> For unto whomsoever much is given, of him shall be much required: and to whom men have committed much, of him they will ask the more.
>
> —Luke 12:48

A Tin Can for the Rich and Famous?

I'm sure of all the billionaires that exist collectively in this country today, none were as rich as King Solomon. Experts have estimated the 100,000 talents of gold and 1,000,000 talents of silver that made up David's temple construction savings account in 1 Chronicles 22:14 to be valued at $63 billion, $40 million in gold and $15 billion, $200 million in silver. This kind of wealth certainly dispels any thought of God not wanting His people rich. But, as it is with all things, there are responsibilities, prerequisites, rules, guidelines, and blueprints required. It is up to us to obey or disobey. So it is with salvation. You can accept it or reject it. Accepting it has its privileges. The same is true with finances. There is great responsibility attached to wealth. As it was with Solomon, so it is with the rich of today. If much is given, much will most certainly be required.

Solomon's story, more than any other world-famous story, involves two appealing resources: wealth and wisdom. I pray that the super rich-rich and famous will take to heart the life of this wealthy king, and that the Holy Spirit will illuminate their minds to realize that being abundantly blessed doesn't make you exempt from God's commandments.

Like many, Solomon inherited his wealth at a young age. His father, King David, was told by God that he couldn't build God's temple, but that his son Solomon would. David referred to Solomon as being young and tender with a great work to accomplish. Solomon's famous temple was the result of his work. So this dispels the idea that the young should not be assigned to oversee great tasks of wealth when God's order and wisdom are sought.

King David (as have others, I'm sure) left his son much wealth to carry on his agenda. David was a great enthusiastic giver in honoring God with the first fruits of all he acquired. He knew and honored the wealth-building principle of the law of reciprocity. He continuously put into practice God's principles of finance, and God saw to it that he acquired enormous wealth. David never lost his focus in honoring God with his best in tithes and offerings, and God rewarded him: "pressed down, shaken and running over" (Luke 6:38). And Solomon accumulated wealth on top of David's wealth.

This wealthy king knew who he was and "whose" he was. He displayed magnificent gratitude and attitude. He was in order, and his tin can (gold-plated, no doubt) overflowed with the riches accumulated from his enemies (the wealthy wicked). Read this poetic account of David in the Word and see if you can feel his heart of thankfulness and honor to God:

> Yours, O Lord is the greatness and the power, and the glory, and the victory, and the majesty; for all that is in the heavens and the earth is Yours; Yours is the Kingdom, O Lord, and Yours it is to be exalted as head over all. Both riches and honor come from You, and You reign overall. In Your hand are power and might; in Your hand it is to make great and to give strength to all. Now therefore, our God, we thank You and praise Your glorious name and those attributes which that name denotes.
>
> But who am I and what is my people, that we should retain strength and be able to offer thus so willingly? For all things come from you, and of Your own (hand) we have given you [tithes and offerings...]. For we are strangers before You, and sojourners, as all our fathers were; our days on the earth are like a shadow, and there is no hope or expectation of remaining.
>
> O Lord our God, all this store [wealth] that we have prepared to build You a house for Your holy name and the token of Your presence comes from Your hand and is all Your own. I know also, my God, that You try the heart, and delight in uprightness. In the uprightness of my heart I have freely offered all these things. And now I have seen with joy Your people, present here,

offer voluntarily and freely to You."
—1 Chronicles 29:11–17, AMP

King David is regarded as a man after God's own heart. Can you see why?

Besides the material wealth David left Solomon, he left wisdom and advice on how to keep the abundance flowing and growing. He beseeched his son to know the God of his father—to have a personal relationship with Him. Look at the advice Solomon's father gave his son in 1 Chronicles 28:9, in which he told him (loosely), "Don't get too big for your britches, lose your riches and end up with stitches."

> And you, Solomon my son, know the God of your father—have personal knowledge of Him, be acquainted with and understand Him; appreciate, heed and cherish Him—and serve Him with a blameless heart and a willing mind. For the Lord searches all hearts and minds, and understand all wondering of the thoughts. If you seek Him—inquiring for and of Him, and requiring Him as your *first* and *vital* necessity, you will find Him; but if you forsake Him, He will cast you off forever!
> —1 Chronicles 28:9, AMP

Did you get that ending? If you forsake or don't honor God, He will forsake and not honor you. So test Him! If you're out of order, He's a merciful God and will forgive. If you don't repent, you will certainly reap what you have sown. It is written that God will not change on your behalf.

Think About It—
Financial fortune without the fear of God will lead to devastation.

King Solomon found this truth to be true. As rich as he

was, he wasn't exempt from God's laws, and neither are you. *Just because you haven't paid today—doesn't mean you won't pay tomorrow.* As God keeps His end of the bargain, so must you. God's promises to men are dependent upon man meeting God's conditions also.

Solomon asked for wisdom at a very early age, and God promised him wealth because of the request. But when Solomon matured, God became quite irate with Solomon because of his degenerate and abominable conduct. He married women who served and worshiped other gods, influencing Solomon to do the same. His heart was filled with treachery against others. His disobedience opened an evil door for trouble to befall him.

So listen, disobedient, out-of-order rich men. I beseech you to honor God with all that He has blessed you with. The price will be more than what you're worth if you don't. One must never get so high and mighty as to abandon God's warnings, rules, guidelines, and commandments. The price will be too hefty to pay. The kingdom that Solomon ruled was stripped from him. God's covenant became null and void due to Solomon's disobedience.

There have been agreements and instructions in God's Word for man's welfare since the beginning of time. There are more instructions in the area of finance than any other subject. Why? *Because financial influence on earth can bring His influence around the earth.* God has always desired for His people to be super-prosperous as long as we acknowledge Him and His Word. As it is written: "Seek *first* the kingdom of God and his righteousness and all these things shall be *added* unto you" (Matt. 6:33, emphasis added). Therefore, it is equally true that if you don't seek first the kingdom of God and His righteousness, all these things shall be *subtracted* from you.

Because Solomon didn't value God's wisdom, his son Rehoboam acted foolishly as he matured. Before Rehoboam's death, the ten northern tribes separated themselves from Judah, and from then on the kingdom went into a downward spiral. Both the north and south kingdoms were utterly destroyed. Why? Solomon broke covenant!

> Then did Solomon build an high place for Chemosh, the abomination of Moab, in the hill that is before Jerusalem, and for Molech, the abomination of the children of Ammon. And likewise did he for all his strange wives, which burnt incense and sacrificed unto their gods. And the LORD was angry with Solomon, because his heart was turned from the LORD God of Israel, which had appeared unto him twice.
> —1 KINGS 11:7–9

Solomon grieved God's kindness by disobeying His law and order, inviting His wrath. Immediately an adversary was raised up to contend with the king. Then a prophet was sent to the son of one of Solomon's servants, promising him the rule of ten of Israel's twelve tribes once Solomon was dead (1 Kings 11:14–37).

God always keeps His promises, but we must keep our promises too. Most Christians and non-Christians alike think God will keep His part of a bargain whether they keep theirs or not. Whatever a man (rich or poor) soweth, that shall he reap (Gal 6:7). There are no exceptions and no exemptions.

As the Word says, "Humble yourselves in the sight of the Lord, and he shall lift you up" (James 4:10). But if you don't humble and return unto Him, He won't lift you up. You have a choice. Salvation works in the same manner. You can be saved if you desire. But if it is not your desire, you most certainly don't have to accept God's salvation.

God wants the best for us, but He loves us enough to allow us the freedom to make our own choices. He doesn't force Himself or His provisions upon anyone. He doesn't want *human robots*. He wants people to

Building Wealth Using the Tin Can Method

come willingly. He is a wonderful gentleman.

Think About It—
It's Your Choice!

Heed These Words of the Lord

Why are you living in luxurious houses while my house lie in ruins? This is what the Lord Almighty says: Consider how things are going for you! You have planted much but harvested little. You have food to eat but not enough to fill you up. You have wine to drink, but not enough to satisfy your thirst. You have clothing to wear, but not enough to keep you warm. Your wages disappear as though you were putting them in pockets filled with holes!

This is what the Lord Almighty says: Consider how things are going for you. Now go up into the hills, bring down timber, and rebuild my house. Then I will take pleasure in it, and be honored says the Lord. You hoped for rich harvest, but they were poor. And when you brought your harvest home, I blew it away. Why? Because my house is in ruins, says the Lord Almighty, while you are busy building your own fine houses.

That is why the heavens have withheld the dew and the earth has withheld its crops. I have called for a drought on your fields and hills...a drought to wither the grain and grapes and olives and all your other crops, a drought to starve both you and your cattle and to ruin everything you have worked so (crookedly) hard to get.

—Haggai 1:4–11, NLT

A TIN CAN FOR THE RICH AND FAMOUS?

PUT GOD'S WORK AT THE TOP!

If God is first in your life then I challenge you to prove it by putting your priorities in order. *Don't fall from riches to stitches!*

Twelve

God's New Upcoming Fortune 500 List

There's a saying about the golden rule—"The man with the gold rules." I like that expression only in the sense that *God owns* all the gold—and He certainly rules (Hag. 2:8). In the secular sense this means whoever has the most money is the one who has the power to get his wishes carried out. But I see many Christians who even believe this, and they are completely out of order with a displaced respect for who is truly in control.

By now I hope you can see the error in this kind of worldly "golden-rule" thinking and the turbulence it has produced in America's financial matters. We have been satisfying the wrong owners. The real owner's rules and guidelines have been violated. No matter how much money the false owner—the impostor, Satan—allows you to make, it will never be sufficient. God, the true ruler, is a God of order, and He has given us His guidelines, which will produce His promised results. There is blessing for the one who heeds His guidelines for success, but a curse for the one who doesn't. The choice is always ours. His loving, gentle nudging will always direct us to His blessings, but He will never force us to obey and walk in His order. Remember, *out-of-order living breeds chaos and turbulence.*

> **THINK ABOUT IT—**
> SATAN, THE IMPOSTOR, IS NOT THE RULER OF AS MANY WEALTHY UNBELIEVERS AS YOU MAY THINK. HE MAY CONTROL TO SOME DEGREE, BUT HE DOESN'T OWN.

You see, there are many seemingly happy wealthy people who have amassed great wealth and truly feel they have reached the "top of the world." But for many, their inward miseries haunt them day and night. There can never be true peace where there is disobedience and unforgiven sin. True godly peace doesn't have a price tag. It lies at the heart of God's blessing, which is not for sale.

Anyone who chooses to remain out of order and rob God creates a self-inflicting curse. Malachi says such a one is cursed with a curse—a double whammy curse. The first curse begins at the point of disobeying God's order and law. The second curse releases the devourer.

Right about now, you may be thinking, *I don't care, lady, what you say; $500,000 would take my worries and cares away.* But I do understand your thinking. When you're in debt or just plain broke, $500,000 would seem like a perfect juicy peach from Georgia heaven. But you must remember: God's Word will never change! What it says is certainly what it means. And if you aren't obeying His orderly laws, just as here in the physical world when you break the natural laws of man, so it occurs in the spiritual realm—you will pay a price. Broken rules and guidelines cost.

Your money, whether little or much, will not be exempt. Neither will it satisfy all of your appetites. You will never be able to make enough money to satisfy all of your needs and greeds. If you make $700,000, you'll require a million. If you make a million, before long you'll need two million to support your lifestyle. You will always be short, even though in the eyes of others you seem to be a success. Only God—and you—will know the truth. Regardless of how much one has, it can't buy health and true happiness.

Recall with me now the story of one of the most famous billionaires of all time: Howard Hughes. With all his wealth, Howard Hughes was a recluse. At the end of his life he was a lonely, miserable man. If money could have bought health and happiness, he would have given everything to obtain them. This is just as true for the person who makes only $50,000 a year. If a curse is upon a person because of disobedience, then insufficiency—never having enough—will also dominate their lives.

Remember, there are just as many poor insufficient rich people as there are insufficient poor people.

THINK ABOUT IT—
REMEMBER—FINANCIAL FORTUNE WITHOUT THE FEAR OF GOD WILL LEAD TO DEVASTATION.

Look at the issue involving the Grammy Award-winning singer-musician-artist, M. C. Hammer, with assets of $9.6 million and debts of $13.7 million. Many of you may be saying, "If I had $9.6 million dollars, I would have.... Or if I had just one million, I would have...." But, again I remind you, if you can't manage to pay God, maintain a savings, and be in order with your $30,000-a-year job, what would cause you to even think you could do it with $9 million?

I believe Hammer will succeed again and be even greater because of what he said in the August 1997 issue of *Ebony* magazine: "My priorities were out of order. My priorities should have always been God, family, community, and business."

So again, being out of order, breeds chaos. May God be with you, M.C. Hammer, to become an example for others in your field who will need you!

Remember, no one is exempt when they're out of order. God keeps His Word and watches over His Word to perform it. Megamillion-dollar athletes, actors, businessmen, and lottery winners are not exempt. So you must follow the GOLDEN RULE of the ONE who truly owns the gold. Or your gold will fail.

GOD'S NEW UPCOMING FORTUNE 500+ LIST

As I briefly mentioned in my introduction, there are currently many anointed men and women who are being raised up to give new revelation to help guide God's people out of financial bondage. As I also said, I believe I am one of them. And I want you to know God is saying there are those who are living according to His order that are going to be enabled to do more with $50 as they sow into the kingdom of God than the disobedient can do with $50,000. God wants to bless His people with miraculous favor to produce financial miracles. He is more than able to deliver unique ways and means of leading His obedient children out of their financial holocaust. He did it with the children of Israel by the rod of Moses, and He will do it for you and I today.

I believe the tables will soon turn on the wealthy wicked. They are soon to find themselves off of the world's Fortune 500 list as God establishes His own. God's Fortune 500+ list will consist of those servants who are obedient and in order.

> Since the zenith of the civil-rights movement, African-American churches have struggled with how to inspire constituents who have been moving into the middle class and away from social-justice issues. The past decade has seen the rise of black "megachurches," huge, middle-class congregations whose pastors preach a "prosperity gospel"—an optimistic message that glorifies personal and economic success while

BUILDING WEALTH USING THE TIN CAN METHOD

shunning the role of victim. . . .

Mr. Jakes is one of the best and most successful of these new prophets; certainly, he is the most visible. His emotional exhortations bring the members of his congregation at the Potter's House, his 16,000-member Dallas church, to tears every week. He is also a shrewd entrepreneur who nurtures, protects and markets his product—himself—with meticulous care.

Mr. Jakes and his ministers use cable and satellite television, direct mail, telephone, magazine columns, workbooks, books, pamphlets, videotapes, audiotapes and the Internet to evangelize. Last year, Mr. Jakes's church brought in revenue of $20.5 million, nearly half of it through sales of videos. "He is a good a businessman as he is a preacher," says Don Nori, chief executive officer of Destiny Image Publishers Inc., which published Mr. Jakes's first book in 1993. "In fact, some might say he's better businessman than he is a preacher."*

More of God's obedient, in-order servants will begin to step onto the worldwide stage, becoming what the world terms an "overnight success." But the actual success will come from their obedience. I believe millions of God's servants will climb from "rags to riches," as the world looks on astonished. The only choice the world will have will be to acknowledge the occurrence as a direct result of the sovereign hand of God.

I believe God will cause the stock prices of many evil corporations to hit rock bottom overnight, never to regain momentum. They won't even know what hit them. Just as the Iron Curtain came down overnight, leaving the world mesmerized by the sudden occurrence, so shall it be for other strongholds that have existed in our lives. Room will be made for many new *witty-invention corporations* that will be spearheaded by God. They will be run by His obe-

---

*Miller, Lisa. 21 August 1998. "Grammy Nomination, Book Deal, TV Spots—A Holy Empire Is Born," *The Wall Street Journal*, vol. 232, no. 37

dient servants to replace the disobedient's corporate slots.

1. The sovereign hand of God will cause money that belongs to His obedient children but which has been seized by Satan to be restored and released.

2. Money that is owed will be repaid; unsaleable property will be unexpectedly sold; prime unbuyable properties will be bought (literally for pennies), and the sellers won't comprehend why they sold them for such meager prices.

3. God's obedient, in-order servants will come out of debt at a rapid rate as a debtless "Jubilee" will take place on behalf of many. Remember, the atomic number for tin is fifty—and fifty is the number that represents God's Year of Jubilee!

Even now, many of these things are happening. I believe they will increase by a greater magnitude. The world's system will be stunned and shaken. Unbelievers will come to be saved when they realize God is real. Those on God's New Fortune 500+ list will be used as a winning tool of salvation for many. The unthinkable, unimaginable, and miraculous will transpire to lead God's servants out of our modern-day Egypt into a modern-day Canaan land!

THINK ABOUT IT—
ONLY GOD CAN AND WILL BALANCE THE SCALES. THUS SAITH THE LORD! THE QUESTION IS: WILL YOU BE IN THAT NUMBER?

Building Wealth Using the Tin Can Method

It Shall Happen

God deeply desires to bless His people, but His order requires our giving *first* so He has something to multiply back to us. Simply put, if you want to insure that your name will show up on God's new Fortune 500+ list, *you're going to have to sow to grow.*

Recall the story of the poor widow who gave all she had, a mere two mites (Mark 12:43–44). Two mites today would be equivalent to a fraction of a penny. That was all she had. It was her entire living, and Jesus proclaimed her giving above all the others. Yet, many of you today may not even possess one mite.

Others have only a small sum such as two mites—and refuse because of embarrassment to give such an amount. Remember the poor widow: God is not concerned with the smallness of your sum. He's interested in your large, obedient heart's willingness to release what you have, just as the widow did with her two mites. I'm sure her offering reaped an abundance, which enabled her to be a "bigger" giver the next time around. She didn't hesitate to give what she had. *She put aside her pride and reaped a prize.*

THINK ABOUT IT—
WITH ALL THAT WAS AND COULD HAVE BEEN RECORDED IN GOD'S WORD, HE WOULDN'T HAVE INCLUDED THE ACCOUNT OF THE WIDOW AND HER TWO MITES IF HE DIDN'T WANT US TO LEARN FROM HER EXAMPLE.

Good Deals

God has also impressed upon my spirit that there will be good deals involving cars, houses, land, miraculous favor, and other things that He will bring before His children—and require mere widow's mites to fully purchase them. Many things are taking place even now. But they will happen in a greater proportions as we reposition ourselves in His order.

"I want to bless you," God is saying today, "but many of My children will have to pass up these blessings. Even though the price will be *small,* they will not even have the small sums that will be necessary to qualify.

"There are many blessings that I am holding that cannot be released, because the people for whom they are intended are out of order and are not ready to receive.

"They must get ready! Some are, but most are not. So many are creating their own delays. The wealth of the wicked is laid up for the just, as My Word says, but the just must be in order for me to transfer it into their hands. Right now, many of the just are out of order and disobedient, and therefore are just as wicked as the wicked according to My Word!

"I will not go against My Word and bless them financially when they have gone against My order and instructions.

"Obedience is the condition of divine blessing," says the Lord.

Obedience will qualify us to get in on God's good deals. He knows where they will be even before they are revealed. He knows who is going to sell before the seller knows he is going to sell. He knows who's going to buy before the buyer buys. God is a discerner of the thoughts and intents of the hearts. So He can cause one to sell and give up what they hadn't planned to provide for God's chosen—and sell for the exact amount of money that is in God's servant's tin can. *No one can orchestrate a deal like the Lord.*

For example, I recall a friend of mine who was having financial problems because the enemy was attacking her family's only mode of transportation. She and her husband had jobs at different locations. They also had three school-age children who required transportation. At that time, I

Building Wealth Using the Tin Can Method

had been personally teaching her about finances and saving. My friend was most obedient toward what she learned and was very willing to apply the knowledge. So God led her to one of His good deals. As He saw her purposing to do what is right according to His Word, He showed her a way of escape from her situation by stepping in and performing the miraculous.

God led my friend to a dealership to look at cars. She thought she was going to buy one of the cars on the lot, make a down payment, and retain a car payment for three to five years, as is the traditional norm. But that wasn't what God had in mind for her. When God opens the door to one of His good deals, He sometimes does the opposite of what our mind perceives He is going to do. So my friend didn't buy one of the cars on the lot. Instead, she bought the car of the secretary who worked for the dealership. The secretary just so happened to be selling her car *unannounced and unadvertised*. And my friend purchased it for a little over $2,000! Even though at the time she didn't have $2,000, God gave her favor in borrowing it—without interest. And guess what...the car was an Audi 500! I think you can classify that as a pretty good deal.

So, get in order, people! When you're in order, God will have a plan laid out for you to walk into with His loving blessings. God knows the where, when, how, and now of every good deal. It gives Him good pleasure to give good gifts to His children; He is no respecter of persons. My friend's obedience provided the miracle. It put her in the right place at the right time with the right deal.

The fact of the matter is, it will make no difference whether or not you know where the deal is or what will completely be taking place. What does matter is that your heavenly Father will know. It works the same way with me and my daughter. It doesn't matter whether she knows where a good deal is as long as I know where it is. Surely I am going to share with her. And that's the way it is with

God. So it makes good sense to be tuned into right fellowship with God. We are required to tune in with our obedience so He can lead us to eat the good of the land.

Tin Can Deals

Now, suppose God has told you about a good deal that He wants you to take advantage of. What if He were to tell you one morning to get up, go two blocks around the corner, and bid or buy this or that? What will you do for money? If you have to go to a bank and borrow, by the time you are finished with the paper work, wait until they check your credit, job status, and references, your good deal may have passed into the hands of another.

We all know that timing is crucial when God says, "Move now!" When He says this, He doesn't mean five days later because of a paperwork holdup. So you will need your tin can ready and waiting to act in a timely manner according to God's instructions. You will need to be ready for action without a waiting period—and without interest.

Remember the free-money fee syndrome I focused on in chapter 9 with which greedy lending institutions are stealing us blind? It costs a fee of $50 or more just to sit down and fill out an application. Your tin can costs you nothing. Now to me, $50 in *your* pocket is better than $50 in *theirs*. After you hand over the $50 fee, they will take out another 1 or 2 percent interest or more on the loan itself.

I often get mental visions in my head about the numerous, endless good deals worldwide that the Lord will bring in the midst of His obedient children. Sometimes they are so overwhelming that I purposefully try to terminate my thoughts because they seem almost unbelievable. When I was having a conversation with a sister in Christ a while back about good deals, she shared the account of a prophet who asked a few in a congregation to give a thousand dollars. The prophet said that by the unction of the Holy Spirit,

Building Wealth Using the Tin Can Method

within that week, witty inventions would come to them from God that would produce millions of dollars.

At that time my mental visions saw the prophets of God being directed by the Spirit to invite hundreds of obedient servants to give, and I saw the ordered and disciplined ones running to the altar. When this happens they will toss in checks and cash before the Lord in the amounts of $5, $10, $20, $50, $100, $1,000, and more. Then the miraculous hand of God will move and produce miracles before they leave the church. Jeremiah 33:3 says, "Call upon me, and I will answer thee, and shew thee great and mighty things, which you knowest not."

Therefore, I ENVISION the hearts of many creditors being moved upon by God. They will call God's people and advise them to declare jubilee upon their indebtedness—even though they don't know why they are suggesting such a thing. (You know this will be a miracle.)

I ENVISION people moving out of their homes and calling to let God's people know that they are relocating and the house is theirs—with no strings attached.

I ENVISION car dealerships that are unable to get rid of enough cars before the end of the season, calling the church to let them know they have hundreds of new cars to give away. They will do this to avoid paying taxes on the unsold inventory.

I ENVISION the lending institutions calling to give God's obedient servants interest-free loans just to borrow their money.

I ENVISION airlines calling obedient and faithful ministers of the gospel to give them airplanes with pilots. These planes and pilots will be at their disposal when they travel to remote countries and islands to spread the gospel. Only a God of the miraculous can cause these things to happen—a God who is omnipotent, omniscient, and omnipresent.

Yes, I ENVISION greater favor, immeasurable favor, unexplainable favor being given to God's servants to go into areas where no person has ever gone before.

I ENVISION these places desiring God's people to come in with the hope of the gospel. It will shake the secular media world because all contact will go to the gospel media.

I ENVISION areas that man never knew existed being discovered by God's chosen only.

I ENVISION angels showing God's chosen ones vast, incomprehensible riches.

I ENVISION God's Word and promises being unfolded in leaps and bounds. And the world will surely know that He is the great I AM. There is none like Him nor shall there ever be. God will display His vast power, His majesty, and His glory. Those who have ears, let them hear.

I believe it shall happen. Yes, all these things will happen and much, much more. God is more than able to accomplish these great things. But again I ask you, dear people, do you believe that He is omniscient, omnipotent, and omnipresent? Do you believe the fullness of the earth is His and all who dwell within it? Either He is the God we serve or He is not. Whose report will you believe?

Conclusion

As I was commissioned daily to write this book, the Lord inspired me repeatedly to address both the woes that are plaguing this land and God's answer to them. At times, Scriptures seemed to come from every direction as my thoughts raced ahead of my hand in writing. The Lord had so much to show me on the subject of financial order that His thoughts bombarded me from time to time. My desire has been to inspire readers to arise to their position in Christ, arising out of any oppression or depression.

In many instances I couldn't connect the various subject matters in relation to the tin can. But as I continued, I began to see how building wealth using the tin can savings method represented obedience and order in simple terms. Simple, yet profound terms.

BUILDING WEALTH USING THE TIN CAN METHOD

You see, tin has a chemical symbol—Sn—and it has the atomic number 50. On May 15, 1948, Israel was declared a nation. As the Word indicates in Leviticus 25:8-13, the Year of Jubilee is at hand; 1998 is the fiftieth year—the year of Jubilee. The symbol of tin—Sn—symbolizes *Starting Now*. Throughout this book I've stressed the need to start now by getting in order, becoming obedient (paying tithes and offerings), as well as starting to save by using the tin can method of saving.

How timely and ironic, don't you think? The atomic number (50) and symbol (Sn) could have been anything other than what it is. I am neither a chemist or scientist, and what chemical symbols and atomic numbers I learned in school lie hidden far back in my memory bank. But God knew it is what would support this message. It is neither *coincidental or accidental*—God deals in neither one.

The tin can message also gives a warning to out-of-order living, which will assuredly produce God's judgment on the disobedient. The simplicity of this message is a call to the young and the old to understand a point of beginning that will allow them to **start now**—right where they are—in giving tithes and offerings and paying themselves. It is a call to you to get in order if you're not, and to remain steadfast if you are to continuously bask under His protection. It is a reminder to remain steadfast in your loyalty to the Lord's written Word and instructions.

It is a call to never surrender to the disobedience of evil because the vindication and ultimate triumph of the Lord is near at hand. As we have seen, the forces of evil often seem increasingly more potent than the powers of good. Yes, the powers that be may possess the most money—for now anyway. They may also possess the most political and social power with all their prestige. But I guarantee you again that they are not the true omnipotent possessors—God is! And God will take your tin can of obedience and fashion miracles before your eyes. He will do it in spite of the government and current financial powerbroker's usury evil because He hasn't forgotten your many acts of kindness (obedience).

The Tables Are Turning

The tables are turning spiritually. You may not recognize it until God removes the scales from your eyes and gives you a glimpse into the spiritual realm. But this is taking place. The oppressed will be set free.

So repent and defray the judgment to come! God's mercy calls for it. As it is written: "If my people, which are called by my name, shall humble themselves, and pray, and seek my face, and turn from their wicked ways; then will I hear from heaven, and will forgive their sin, and will heal their land" (2 Chron. 7:14). If our nation won't call upon God and repent, our prayers will bring forth His judgment. But our prayers will make the difference.

Weep and Howl

The apocalyptic words of James 5:1–6 expresses the remorse and terror of this coming judgment:

> Look here, you rich [wicked, disobedient, out-of-order] people, weep and groan with anguish because of all the terrible troubles ahead of you. Your wealth is rotted away, and your fine clothes are moth-eaten rags. Your gold and silver has become worthless. The very wealth you were counting on will eat away your flesh in hell. This treasure you have or accumulated will stand as evidence against you on the day of judgment. For listen! Hear the cries of the field workers who you have cheated of their pay. The wages you held back cry out against you. The cries of the reapers have reached the ears of the Lord almighty. You have spent

Building Wealth Using the Tin Can Method

> your years on earth in luxury satisfying your every whim. Now your hearts are nice and fat, ready for the slaughter. (The time has come and is here today). You have condemned and killed good people who had no power to defend themselves against you.
> —James 5:1–6, NLT

The tin can message is also a warning and a call to the greedy rich. God loves you and desires your repentance to avoid His wrath to come. When you wake up, God will use you in eternal matters.

This book is a call to God's people to take control of their lives by ordering themselves right with God's Word and His ways. You, Christian believer, must take control over your financial situation so you can be prospered by God to assist in spreading the gospel to those who are lost and entrapped in Satan's web. Who else *can* do it? Who else *will* do it? And, who else *should* do it? God has plans and strategies that will enable you to assist in setting the captives free, but it takes money. Lots and lots of money. And you won't have it to give unless you follow God's instructions. God is only obligated to bless and prosper you according to how you obey.

The covenant blessing of God was given to Abraham and his seed, which includes you and me. God's omniscient plan is to bless us in every area of our lives to make those who are lost in the world marvel at our prosperity.

The world needs to know that there's only one true and just God, and that when He blesses and prospers, it comes without sorrow.

> The blessing of the Lord, it maketh rich, and he addeth no sorrow with it.
> —Proverbs 10:22

There are no evil, negative, or satanic strings attached to

God's prosperity. It saddens me to see Satan's manipulative financial schemes so accepted today. It saddens me even more when God's people play right into his hands. Allow the Holy Spirit to enlighten your understanding and give you spiritual eyes to see and ears to hear. There's nothing new under the sun, including Satan and his manipulative schemes.

Because this book deals with finances, I have only expounded on that subject. But know and understand that the area of finances is *one* of the devourer's *main hidden agendas*. He seeks to control this area of our lives to control the world's financial system. But praise God, it won't happen. This book and others will be a wake-up call for many—and Satan knows it. He has fought me hard in many areas to stop it from coming forth. But the fact that you are reading it proves he didn't have the last hoorah. The fact that you are reading this book is also evidence that his plots are being destroyed. Greater is He that is within me than he that is in the world!

Satan knows that man can be appeased by attractive and beautiful things that appear pleasurable, like money or wealth. That's why he has been so successful in controlling the masses of his dark kingdom through luring them to use unscriptural means to accumulate it. This includes selling drugs, pornography, gambling, crooked politics, television, and yes, not paying tithes and offerings.

We must set ourselves in a positive position to receive financial miracles from God through obeying His Word. Satan will never cease creating and manipulating the world's monetary system, which boasts great power to bring forth his plan. And we shouldn't expect him to. Revelation 13 says it will finally come to a point that no one will be able to buy or sell without taking Satan's special mark. This is a spiritual battle, and until then we have a God who rebukes the devourer when we obey God's plan. So we don't stand alone in this war against Satan. Ordered, obedient Christians are destined to rule this land.

Building Wealth Using the Tin Can Method

Do It God's Way

I want to leave you with one final example of the importance of God's order, which shows the kind of precision God expects when it comes to obeying His Word. It involves David's removal of the ark of the covenant in 1 Chronicles 13–15. Before David recovered the ark of the covenant from Abinadab's house, he consulted with his captains and cabinet ministers. Then he consulted with the congregation. But he made a grave mistake. David consulted everyone except the "the Leader" Himself. In fact, he shouldn't have gone to anyone except God first. Why? Order. When the ark was constructed, God commanded Moses to make sure that only Levites carried it. Yet David didn't consult God's Word. David announced, "If it seems good unto you ("you" or "them"—not "God"), and if the Lord our God let us, send abroad and bring again the ark of our God to us."

Before I fully understood the importance and power of order, I thought that since David had consulted with his leaders it was okay, and that since they were all in agreement, he had obediently fulfilled the Scripture that says, "There is safety in the multitude of counseling." But I finally came to realize there is only safety in the multitude of *wise* counseling—if others are to be consulted at all. Many counselors and counseling sessions aren't wise unless they seek to know God's order, and not one of David's advisors in this case directed the congregation to seek the Word of God. So when a well-meaning Hebrew by the name of Uzza put forth his hand to hold the ark to keep it from falling off the ox cart on which David had placed it, God's anger smote him to death.

> And when they came unto the threshingfloor of Chidon, Uzza put forth his hand to hold the ark; for the oxen stumbled. And the anger of the LORD was kindled against Uzza, and he smote him, because he put his

> hand to the ark: and there he died before God.
> —1 Chronicles 13:9–10

When I first read this, I was really bent out of shape. I recall putting the Bible down in disbelief, feeling very confused and wondering how God could be so cruel when the Word says God is Love. But since that time I have come into the knowledge of God's order through His written Word and the guidance of the Holy Spirit. I steadily began to realize that because of their *disobedience,* they suffered the consequences, because God doesn't change; He is immutable.

David did discover God's order (as I hope many of you have now that we are at the end of this book), and he was wiser the second time around. Notice what the Scripture says when David pitched a tent for the ark in Jerusalem and gave instructions concerning it:

> And David called for Zadok and Abiathar the priests, and for the Levites, for Uriel, Asaiah, and Joel, Shemaiah, and Eliel, and Amminadab, and said unto them, Ye are the chief of the fathers of the Levites: sanctify yourselves, both ye and your brethren, that ye may bring up the ark of the Lord God of Israel unto the place that I have prepared for it. *For because ye did it not at the first, the Lord our God made a breach upon us, for that we sought him not after the due order.* So the priests and the Levites sanctified themselves to bring up the ark of the Lord God of Israel.
> —1 Chronicles 15:11–14, emphasis added

Think About It—
The intentions of David and Israel were good and commendable, but good ideas and God ideas aren't one and the same.

Building Wealth Using the Tin Can Method

God didn't want Uzza to die. But he was out of order. He wasn't a Levite, the ark wasn't being carried by Levites on poles, and Uzza touched the holiness of the Lord. These people went against God's pre-written order when they should have known better. You can't build any house that will stand if you don't have a blueprint to follow. Just like the foundation, the house is doomed to fall if it doesn't have a solid foundation. And the foundation is *order.*

As long as David followed God's guidelines he was successful. But when he did things his own way, he failed miserably.

At the heart of the tin can message is learning to obey the disciplined order of God's financial ways and the positives or negatives that will result through our decisions. When you do things your way, you will fail, too. But when you get in the kind of disciplined order that God is calling you to, you will succeed and overcome the world. Malachi 3:10 is God's rule of order for you and me. So I implore you once more to trust and obey.

> Bring ye all the tithes into the storehouse, that there may be meat in mine house, and prove me now herewith, saith the Lord of host, if I will not open you the windows of heaven, and pour you out a blessing, that there shall not be room enough to receive it.
> —Malachi 3:10

God is a God or order, and He highly regards obedience.
The Word says that "obedience is better than sacrifice"—especially when it comes to your finances. So follow God's blueprint, instructions, and commands, and His blessings will surely overtake you. Build your foundation to wealth by paying your tithes and offerings—*you* bring them to the storehouse.

All of Satan's inspired fee schemes are unjustifiable and immoral. Yes, our government system gives many companies and financial institutions Satan's license to steal. But it won't matter when God has rebuked the devourer on your behalf and broken every curse over your finances. Satan's powers are currently having their "heyday." They're making their hay while the sun still shines. But God has planned His own special "pay day" for them. In the meantime, God's obedient, ordered servants who obey His covenant will be blessed regardless of the "hook" and "crooks" of Satan's worldly scheme. As it was for Jacob when his father-in-law Laban who deceived him reneged on his original promise, we too will reap bountifully in the land, and come out with the wicked's riches (Gen. 30:31).

Get in line with Malachi 3. Then pay yourself in your tin can (that I hope has already received many dollars since you picked up this book) and watch God bring all kinds of blessings, prosperity, and miraculous favor into your life and into the lives of your families. Watch your little change graduate to a lot of change. Watch the favor of God come along with good deals. You won't understand it or be able to explain it—but it will happen! The blind man whom Jesus healed in John 9:25 attested, "All I know is that once I was blind and now I can see." All you will know is that yesterday you were in lack, and today you are blessed.

Don't reject God's Word or His plan for your financial deliverance. Recognize and admit your problem; then replace that problem with "God's financial plan" and your tin can. As you get in God's order, your needs will be supplied abundantly. You will be blessed with an enormous overflow to help finance the End-Time harvest that is happening now in the world. **MAY GOD RICHLY PROSPER YOU** as you build your wealth using the tin can method. It works!